get good

at

PRESENTING

get good at PRESENTING

The no-nonsense guide to authentic and engaging public speaking

Lee Jackson

Copyright © Lee Jackson

ISBN 978-0-9567542-8-8

The right of Lee Jackson to be identified as the author of this work has been asserted by him in accordance with the Copyrights, Designs and Patents Act 1988.

First published 2018.

All rights reserved.

No part of this publication may be reproduced or transmitted in any form or by any means, electronic or mechanical, including photocopy, recording or any information storage and retrieval system, without permission in writing from the publisher.

Published by Engaging Books

Design and typesetting by Ashdown Creative

All photos, slides and diagrams copyright © Lee Jackson unless stated otherwise

Disclaimer:
All information in this book is correct and safe to use as far as we were able to establish, but please be sensible and always take precautions when changing or adding software to your computer. We cannot be held responsible for problems with your computer and cannot answer direct questions of a technical nature, please consult your I.T. Department, local PC shop or techie friend for help. We really believe that the information here will transform your presentations but we also cannot be held responsible if your talk goes badly and you don't get that promotion or new account you went for!

LeeJackson.biz

Dedication

For Linda and Baz, two of the bravest
and best communicators I know.

"This book will bring comfort to the 99.9% of us who see presentations and speaking as a learnable skill rather than something that the other 0.1% are born with.

It is about three Cs. Giving the reader the competence, commitment and confidence to inspire others through the spoken word."

Phil Jesson, Former Head of Speaker Development, Academy For Chief Executives

"Read this book and you will get good, guaranteed. It does what it says on the tin....except it's a book."

John Archer, Top Comedy Magician and Two Time BAFTA Winner

"Lee Jackson has already made a valuable contribution to the world by helping speakers to stop using PowerPoint badly. Now he turns his attention to helping speakers with their whole presentation, from preparation to delivery, handling Q&A's to getting feedback and handling anxiety. In his characteristic no-nonsense style, Lee gives you everything you need to make your next speech a masterpiece. I highly recommend this book."

Graeme Codrington, Futurist, Author and Professional Speaker

"Warning: only read this book if you are hard enough to take the truth about presentations. Jackson destroys all the old myths and provides a vigorous vaccine for the PowerPoint Plague. This is not merely a gem: it's a game changer."

Graham Davies, Bestselling Author of "The Presentation Coach"

"When it comes to presenting Lee Jackson has been there, done that and got the t-shirt. Which is why this book is invaluable. It's written by someone with both expertise and experience and that's what makes it one of the best you'll read on the subject."

Paul McGee, International speaker and bestselling author of SUMO (Shut Up, Move On) and Self Confidence

"Lee Jackson is a speaker I've heard many times and he never fails to inspire me. Whether you feel like you are just starting out as a speaker in business or you have been at it for years I recommend you read this book to help you raise your game and advance your career!"

Matt Bird, International speaker & founder of Relationology

"Lee Jackson has the rare ability to help people communicate professionally both verbally and visually. This book will be an invaluable guide for anyone who needs to make presentations – which is just about everyone!"

Alan Stevens, Past President, Global Speakers Federation

"The ability to present your ideas effectively is fast becoming a vital skill…which is where Lee comes in. Lee has an uncanny knack of taking the twaddle out of presentation theory. He's a Presentation Sherpa that not only knows all the traps and pitfalls but takes great pleasure in sharing some very clever ways to navigate around them. I've had the pleasure of seeing him selflessly share his insight and expertise on stage (and yes, he really does practice what he preaches) and seen the huge impact it has on his audiences."

Simon Morton, CEO of Eyeful Presentations and author of 'The Presentation Lab'

"I love it! It tells us exactly what to do, but more importantly 'HOW' to do it! Simple, easy to apply techniques that will make us all better presenters, including content structure, managing nerves, powerpoint and so much more. A GREAT book!"

David Hyner, Researcher and Speaker

"Lee knows his stuff and here he's upfront about how to excel up front. Learn from the master!"

Paul Kerensa, Comedian/Writer (BBC's Miranda, Top Gear)

Acknowledgments

A heart-felt thanks to everyone who has contributed so generously to this book, either as crowd-funders, contributors, influencers, encouragers, advisors and friends – specifically – Ann Page, Peter Smith, Frederika Roberts, Toby White, Michelle Mills-Porter, Andy Lenton, Ian Wilson, Duncan Stow, Tim Cobham, Julie Holmes, Keith & Trish Fearnley, Frowa Schuitemaker, Pete Lawrence, Jonathan Eastwood, Lesley Flynn, Mike Gibbons, Ian F Barlow, Julie Creffield, Pearl Jordan, John Burns, Penny Haslam, Jacqueline Scargill, Steve Pepper, Jeremy Nicholas, Alan Stevens, Graeme Codrington, Pam Burrows, John Archer, Tim Vine, Jo Enright, Geoff Ramm, Joan Freeman, Chris Schorah, Helen Schofield, Stuart Gregg, Suzi Irwin, Garr Reynolds, Nancy Duarte, Dayspring, Niels Brabandt, Neil McCoy-Ward, Steve Bustin, Joy Marsden, Adam Braimah, Pip Wilson, The PSA, The NSA, Karen C. Eddington, John B. Molidor, Guy Clapperton, Lee Warren, Pippa White, Andie Wilson, Bryony Thomas, my amazing family and anyone I may have forgotten. I would also like to particularly mention Paul McGee, Steve McDermott, Phil Hesketh, Curly Uppington, Dave Hyner, Peter Roper, Mike Pagan, John Hotowka and Richard McCann who really encouraged me in the early days.

Thank you.

Contents

"The art of communication
is the language of leadership."
James Humes

Introduction

"Ladies and gentlemen, I give to you the groom Mr. Lee Jackson!" This was probably my best speech – it felt great and was on the biggest day of my life. I remember starting with the classic line "Unaccustomed as I am to public speaking" and that got a laugh and a few heckles – mainly because even then I was 'very accustomed' to public speaking – I had spoken to thousands of people in that year alone. It was a good tongue in cheek first line though. And *shock horror* I did all of my wedding speech without a single powerpoint slide. Your opening line is important. Of course at my wedding the audience were engaged from the start and probably would have been whatever I said.

Obviously, there are many different types of businesses and job roles, but in my experience, most, if not all of them involve some sort of presenting or speaking. That may be a regular team talk, hosting a conference, a sales pitch or just presenting a new proposal. Even though we all have to do it, the reality is – we rarely get the help or training to do it well, a bit like parenting.

The irony of this is that people who present well, often do well and go further.

It's hard to think of a leader from the last 70 years who wasn't a great presenter in some way. Every leader has to learn to present well as they know this is how to influence people, from Bob Geldof banging the desk on live TV at Live Aid when people weren't giving enough money, through to Mother Theresa at the United Nations in 1985. The UN

Secretary General introduced the 4'11" Albanian nun as "the most powerful woman in the world". Leaders have to communicate well.

If you present well it will help your career, your organisation and will help you to move forward, yet still people don't get trained in it. I find that a bit odd.

I was invited to a conference as a delegate with eight speakers a few years ago, but all I remember about the day is the lack-lustre venue, coffee, and that the presentations were so forgettable! They all gave us death by PowerPoint, and very dull presentations. There were 250 bored people in the room and I thought – what a waste of everyone's time. People left early, and checked their emails during the talks.

Time is really precious, it's the one thing we can't ever get back. Presentations don't have to be time-wasting. We can be engaging, we can make an audience laugh, or at the very least smile. We can be ourselves, we can be professional, and we can be memorable. That's how to get ahead in business. That's how we can get organisations to change. We can engage an audience and make them think 'Ah that was the speaker that made me think/laugh/change my behaviour.' That's what we should be aiming for.

Why me writing this book?

I was the 2017 President of the Professional Speaking Association in the UK & Ireland. But more importantly, I am a pro speaker. I speak for a living, it's how I pay my bills, it is what I do. For the last 10 years I have been speaking full-time in businesses, schools, colleges – in fact, all sorts of places. I do my talks in many different environments, some more challenging than others, like prisons and secure units. I have learned through necessity how to engage with reluctant audiences and how to get to the point quickly. I have learned how to recover a conference after a bad speaker and how to set up everything on my own without a red carpet or someone to help me. I have learned the hard way and have had to deliver often against the odds. I wouldn't have it any other way, so rather than keep anything I've learnt to myself, I thought I'd share with you, here.

So here are some of the tips and tricks that I have learned along the way. This isn't a huge book with long, complicated academic communication theories, it's down to earth, practical and concise, and hopefully it will make a big impact on the way that you present and how you engage with audiences.

Dip in, dip out.

Enjoy.

Don't hide behind your slides

When you are using corporate slides, templates, or the slides that your boss gave you, you are, in effect hiding behind those slides. Perhaps you don't have confidence in your speaking, or you're thinking "if I can just use the slides I somehow don't have to show my personality".

Great speakers are authentic and allow their personality to come out in their talks. People want to connect with people, it's what presentations are all about – person to person. It's never primarily about a spreadsheet – that stuff comes later with handouts. First we have to pitch, and get our idea across – an idea for your business or an idea that will change the world.

Don't hide behind your slides. Great speakers are comfortable in their own skin. They are people who just say look this is me, this is who I am, this is what I do, this is the company I work for, this is the charity that I run, this is me. That's what I have done most of my life, it's kind of scary at times but there is no way round it, we have to be ourselves. Don't hide behind your suit, or hide behind your slides, let the authentic you really shine out and I guarantee you will get better feedback. You will make more of a difference and if you are in business I am pretty sure you will make more profit too.

I stand at the front and say "Hello my name is Lee Jackson. I am motivational speaker and what you see is what you get. I will be the same person on stage as I will be at the coffee break, except slightly more interesting on stage with some funnier stories and different content!".

It's that idea that you can be the same person on and off stage that people respect and that is what makes a difference. Most of my great feedback is from people saying "oh you were just you, you were normal, you were authentic, you seemed approachable". These are things that I have worked on and developed my character about, because why would I want to be anyone else, that's the reality.

Don't play hide and seek, learn to become you, the authentic you.

That makes all the difference.

How do you feel when you are presenting?

Maybe you have never done a speech before, maybe you've only done a quick talk at school or University. Most of us have done a talk at least once in our life, there will be very few people reading this that have never done a talk at all.

Let me ask you a question – how do you feel when you speak in front of people?

Imagine you've been asked to give a presentation tomorrow afternoon.

How do you feel about that?

Stop and think now.

What is going through your mind?

Are you thinking who will be in the audience? Do you feel more anxious or nervous if it will be people that you know or if it's going to be complete strangers? Would the subject of the presentation be a big issue for you?

If you could speak about something you know really well is that easier for you than speaking about something that you don't know about?

What makes you feel more comfortable?

What makes you feel more uncomfortable?

On the whole, you hopefully get to speak about what you know and in fact I would always turn down a talk that isn't in my field of expertise. Don't do a talk about something that you don't know about. I get lots of requests to speak and some of them I turn down because even if I am free that day and it would be nice to earn some money, I still say no unless it's directly related to my main knowledge.

If you are at a party and someone says, "What do you do?" you can probably speak for 3 or 4 minutes about your job without even thinking about it. If you are really passionate about your job it might be 30 minutes without even thinking about it, so speaking is never usually a problem, its ***public*** speaking that is.

The issue is that when we get up front we start overthinking everything.

Overthinking is a real problem for many people.

We panic in our heads and catastrophise easily, thinking of the worst instead of the best. "Oh no what if they do this?" "What if this doesn't work?" "What if this isn't going to happen?" "What if they all know more than I do?" "What if I am speaking to someone who has been in a similar role for 25 years" "What if they hate me?" "What if I [add your particular public speaking fear here!]".

These are all things we can overthink but ultimately when you know about your subject it should make it easier for you to speak on it. All it requires is for us to deal with our overactive brain, do some good preparation, and tweak our delivery style – then I guarantee it will be a lot better than you think.

Speaking from the front can be one of the most rewarding and fulfilling life experiences we have. It just needs a little work to get us to a level of confidence so that we can enjoy it.

That's what this book of tips and tricks is all about, whether you are a seasoned pro or a nervous newbie, let me help you.

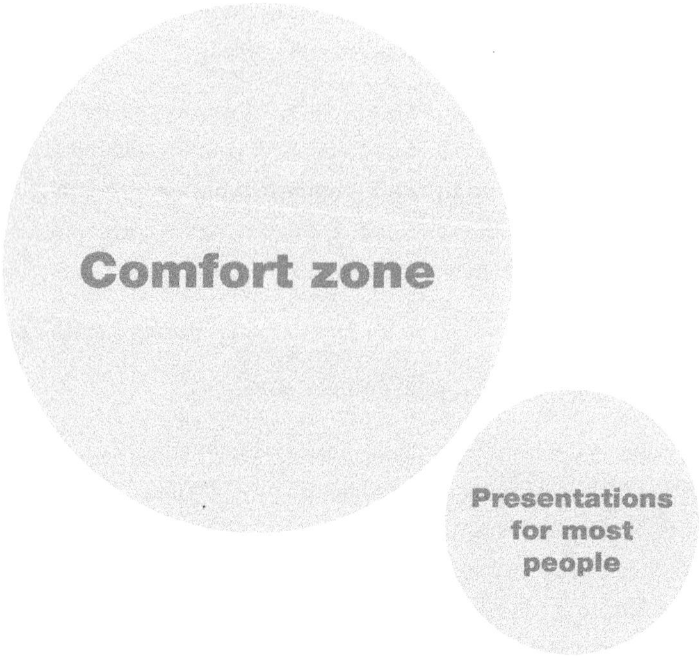

Comfort zone

Presentations for most people

In reality this is where presentations sit for most people. Development and learning doesn't take place in our comfort zone, it takes place when we push out the boat from the shore, and then when we get out of the boat and start stepping onto the water! In other words we have to step out, we have to try something new to learn something new. My comfort zone is probably my lounge at home watching a film, or some comedy with a nice cup of tea, and I might learn bits from there occasionally but that's not where Lee Jackson gets developed – that's where I go to relax.

To develop requires me to move out of my comfort zone.

For 99% of people that's where presentations fit – outside their comfort zone.

Even if someone says to you "I don't get nervous doing a presentation" they are probably lying, or they are saying that so that they can control their anxiety. If they voice their nervousness then they'll start saying to themselves "I feel nervous" "I feel nervous". Saying they are not nervous probably helps them not to be nervous, if you understand what I mean.

Let's step out together.

Is it a skill or a talent?

Do you think people are born good speakers or do you think they develop it over time?

I think it is a more complex question than it first seems.

When I was younger I used to think it was a talent, I grew up listening to some great talks. One of my teenage heroes was Martin Luther King Jnr. and listening to the 'I have a Dream' speech aged 15 I thought "wow that guy must have been born like that". To hold all those thousands of people in the palm of his hand and to speak like he does, almost singing. To be that eloquent surely that must be a talent. Then again when I think about Martin Luther King Jnr. or Barack Obama I realise of course that from an early age they were taken to a black majority church. Most weeks they would be hear fantastic speakers engaging an audience for over an hour, with great use of tone and volume. Hearing that over and over again must have had an impact. No matter what your politics I still think that Barack Obama is a great speaker. Was he born like that? Well of course he wasn't born like that, he saw speakers lots and lots of times and probably started getting up to speak when he was in high school. At University he started getting time on his feet too.

It is time on the stage that makes the difference.

I spent a lot of my life listening to my Dad. My Dad who has passed away now, was a vicar and most weeks I'd to go to church and he would be doing the talk. I would get dragged to big conferences too with my Mam and Dad and would hear great talks, sometimes sleeping on the back row of the audience as the night wore on! So, I wonder now what effect that had on me. I remember one guy in particular called Tony Campolo – he is an Italian-American preacher and he was amazing. I was at a festival with my parents and about 10,000 other people. He was on a big main stage and I remember hearing him speak with such passion, when in the middle of his talk the PA system broke down. Even though there were thousands of people there, he didn't stop. He just said in his American accent "I don't need a mic you can still hear me!!" and he just went for it, he didn't even need a PA system or a microphone and we heard every word that he said.

So, yes, it's a skill you can develop. Listen to as many talks as you can – you can look up some Ted Talks online. Look up other styles too, because Ted is a particular style. Go and see people live, even if you don't agree with them, go and see professional speakers, go on courses and get yourself out there so you can practice and also see how others do it.

One of my hobbies is watching comedy and so we will talk about comedy a bit in this book as I try to inject a little bit of humour here and there, but I urge you to go and see lots of stand-up comedy because I know that we can learn so much from it. If you can, watch Robin Williams 'Live at the Met', probably the best comedy set of all time in my opinion. Just watch how he presents, it's not how you should be of course, it's not how I should be, but there are elements that we can learn from and see only by **purposefully** looking at good practice.

So, is it a skill or is it a talent? If it's a talent then just put this book down now and walk away, but I guarantee you it's a skill.

I will try to get you to a place where you are confident enough or more confident than you are now to get up front and from that time you will start to develop your skills and confidence in front of an audience.

Communication is one of life's best skills to have.

A bad political speech can teach us a lot

In 2014 UK MP Liz Truss spoke at the Conservative Party Conference, she was at the time the minister for the environment, food and rural affairs. She gave what is often seen as possibly one of the worst speeches ever made at a UK political conference.

There is a link to it from my book resources page here: http://bit.ly/GetGoodPresExtras

The reason why it was so bad is because it seemed that she had been over-coached – she was told when to pause, when to smile, and even her smile didn't look right – it looked forced. The pauses seemed forced, the whole thing was odd and disjointed.

The idea is to be yourself up there so you don't have to do a fake smile, you don't have to think "I need to pause now" because as you practise the pauses will come at the right moments.

Find your own style of speaking and let's develop that as we progress.

If you want to develop your presentation skills you should look at three main areas.

1. Preparation (of your material)

2. Delivery (on stage)

3. Anxiety (before, during and after speaking)

I will cover these three in this book.

As some of you may know I have also written a book called

'PowerPoint Surgery' and so I should probably cover slides too in the preparation of your material.

Why slides as well?

Well, because they can be all encompassing. I have had people come to my course and listen to me for a whole day, do exercises and grow in their confidence and then right at the end of the day say to me that they can't change much because they feel drawn back to their slides at all times. I want to put them into context because we have got to move away from our slides and learn how to prepare and deliver **BEFORE** we ever open up Microsoft PowerPoint, Apple Keynote or any other program that you use.

A great speaker isn't a good set of slides, it's you.

Before we start thinking about preparation it's good to understand a little bit about how you're made up.

What's your personality type, how do you deal with talk planning?

The way I see it there is a scale.

On one end of the scale is 'winging it', turning up not even thinking about it, making it up as you go along. I've heard people say "I never prepare talks I just get up there and see what happens".

I was shocked – "Really? You do that?!"

I mean we can all 'wing it' to a certain extent but over the other end of the spectrum is over planning /and perfection obsession – where people become a little OCD about the planning and they spend 20 hours preparing a five-minute talk.

It happens.

So we have got to be careful.

Whether we are at one end or the other, we must be careful because there are dangers at both extremes.

Where **are** you on the scale?

Where **should** you be on the scale?

Where **would** you really like to be on the scale?

Do you like to 'wing it' a bit? Are you good in the moment or are you better when you know exactly what you are going to say? The scale changes as you get older, it changes as you get more experience, these things are not set in stone. I am definitely good at 'winging it' and being in the moment, but actually I plan a lot too.

I was sad when Robin Williams the comedian died. The good to come out of that though is I learned a bit more about him they showed documentaries about him and a lot of the old comedy routines too. I saw an interview with him and he talked about the way that he got ready to do his stand-up gigs. He said that what he does is he plans lots of stuff. He is in his dressing room, planning and thinking about it but then he puts the plan down and he goes out and performs it. I thought that's what I do, because I do plan, I like to do research and I make sure my preparation is good. I'm reading around the subject, reading blogs and news but ultimately I realise that I just need to get out and perform it, because I am good 'in the moment'. So that's where I am on the scale I am probably somewhere in the middle leaning towards winging it, but if I'm not careful I can drift to the unhelpful over-planned side too.

If it's a work talk where would you be on the scale?

If it's a personal talk like a wedding speech where would you be?

Preparation

"WIIFM??!!"

That's what the audience is screaming at speakers, whenever anyone stands up front, whether it's me as a professional or whether it's a new speaker – people are asking the question "What's In It For Me?"

'WIIFM'

They're asking the question "why should I listen to you?"

"What on earth is in this for me?"

Sometimes they are asking it quietly or sometimes they are screaming it in their heads – "why should I give up my time to listen to this person?".

Sometimes when I'm with organisations – the leadership team want me to be there but the staff don't know who I am, they've just got dragged out of the office for the day and they hope they are going to get some nice food. Then this bloke from Yorkshire stands up "a so-called called Motivational Speaker".[1]

So, I've got to answer that **'WIIFM'** question pretty quickly and I try to answer it in the first few minutes.

Answer it well and it changes everything, the audience suddenly go "Oh I see, that's what he is going to help me with!".

You can say obvious things like "by the end of this talk I want to make this happen…", "I want to help you to understand this…", "I am going to help you with this…". Those are the things that really matter because once people have bought into it, once they have understood "oh right I get that" then you will find you can actually see that in their faces. You can see the buy-in in their eyes and their shoulders, they sit up in their chairs and their shoulders become less slumped and they go "Ok, right I will give this guy a chance", "I'll give him 20 minutes and see what he comes up with!"

Think, right from the beginning, how are you going to answer **'WIIFM'**?

If you get that right in the planning stages you are halfway there with engagement.

1. I do have the worst job title in the world! Can you imagine being introduced at a party as a motivational speaker people usually say immediately "oh go on then motivate me". But that's what I call myself because it is what I do and that's what people Google and that's how you get the work, it's a new world of weird job titles! Being introduced as a motivational speaker can also put people on the back foot because I turn up at these events at a staff day, they have had a nice lunch and they put me on after lunch, which is one of my favourite slots of the day because I am pretty lively so I don't mind dealing with that, just don't put the finance person on after lunch in my experience otherwise people fall asleep, after having their sponge pudding.

Start with the end in mind

One of the most influential personal development books ever is The 7 Habits of Highly Effective People® by Dr. Stephen Covey. The book is so influential that his 7 habits are now in everyday usage – like 'win-win' and put 'first things first'.

'Habit' 2 is 'begin[2] with the end in mind' and for speech writing that is key. This is great advice.

Don't just dive in and start getting ready to say all you know about the subject but think – what is the purpose of my talk?

What do I want people to walk away with at the end of my talk?

So you may want A, B, and C, but not only that – what's the core of your message?

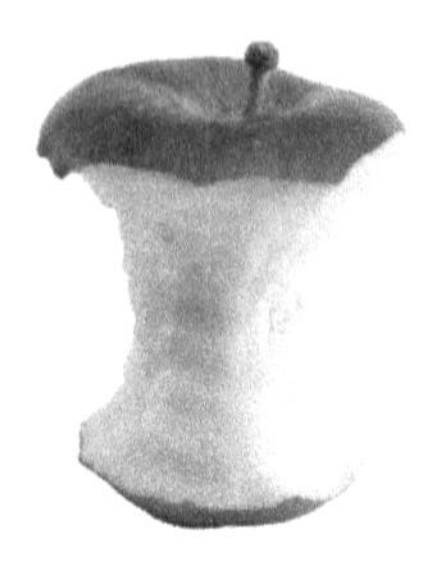

What is the take-away?

In other words, what you really want people to understand.

2. Or start – as I tend to say

Boring talks are usually because people tell you everything that they know.

So if they are doing a customer service talk they will tell everything they know about customer service and share the thousands of pieces of data they've collected and the 25 stories they have heard and the things that they have put in place, all in 20 minutes. Ouch.

I do quite a bit of work in the health sector and I help clients to develop some of the induction training. One of the things they have to do is help people to remember to wash their hands properly. Pretty simple. People need to wash their hands which then helps to stop the spread of infections. Easy. Now as a man I can tell you that many, many times I have been in a men's toilet and found men coming out of the cubicle and walking straight out of the door without washing their hands – it is as gross as it gets. They even walk past the signs that says, "now wash your hands". In hospitals of course, it's doubly important that they do this. Now, in the training talk they can talk about infections, they can list all the infections that not washing your hands can spread. They can talk about the effect on a patient, but what actually is the core message what they want people to walk away with? It is to wash your hands after going to the toilet and **before** they touch a patient and **after** they touch a patient. That's what they want people to walk away with – so the data and everything else is all very nice but really they want people to change behaviour. Simple.

Most talks are about changing behaviour, we want people to think differently about a subject and we want to challenge their preconceptions. We want them to think differently about themselves or maybe about their business. They can only do this when we have our message clear.

So, get to the core of your message, it changes everything.

The way that we plan changes the way we deliver.

Death by PowerPoint is usually people cutting and pasting every piece of information they have without understanding their core message or without starting with the end in mind.

The result is boredom and ineffective communication.

One good way of getting to the core quickly is to ask the “why?” question.

So, ask “why is it me doing this talk?”, not “Oh no why me?!” I don’t mean that.

I mean why you, why this talk, why this audience, why at this time, why these people, why at that time of the day etc etc. If you ask the why question enough like two year olds do, on and on and on, you will find that you get to the core of your message.

The other question you can ask is the “so what?” question. I have seen that done many times – where people say something about their presentation and coaches say “so what?” and keep saying “so what?” and keep saying “so what?” until the presenter sharpens their topic and gets to the core of what they want to say. I saw this seemingly harsh process transform someone’s business model once, they suddenly ‘got’ what they offered others and changed their approach because of it, they got to the core of what they did.

Once you do that it changes everything and makes your job so much easier.

Learn to frame your talk

Putting a frame around your talk, putting it into context also helps you at the preparation stage. Talks don't exist in some kind of abstract world, they are not like a Jackson Pollock painting of seemingly random paint splashes on a blank canvas. They exist within a frame.

They are for a specific purpose or a specific task at a specific time for a specific group of people.

Generic talks don't really work, we have got to think about the frame they are in.

Imagine you are putting a picture frame around your talk, ask who is it for, where is it going to be and for what reason?

Let the answers to the 'Why?' questions frame your talk.

Then when you have got the real frame for your talk you can start to put pen to paper and start doing your preparation.

Fake news is real!

Before you prepare let me just give you a warning, don't believe everything you hear, whether it is from colleagues, speakers, trainers, or just friends you have heard say something.

Don't believe everything you hear because what they have said may simply not be true.

Don't believe everything that the internet says either – just because it is on an Instagram meme or because you have seen it in on one of these posters people put on their kitchen walls doesn't mean that it's actually true.

For instance:

> "Shoot for the moon. Even if you miss, you'll land among the stars."
>
> **Brian Littrell**
>
> **(Formerly of The Backstreet Boys!)**

Well, as lovely a quotation as it is and as much of a fan as I may be of the aforementioned Backstreet Boys, (Backstreet's back, alright) actually the moon is 238,856 miles away from earth and the nearest star is Proxima Centauri which is about 4.22 light-years from Earth and is our closest star other than the sun. So Brian maybe a great singer and these words maybe on greetings cards, memes and kitchen walls worldwide – but, it's simply not true.

We must do our research well at the preparation stage, and not repeat things that people have repeated over the years.

Myths get propagated and unfortunately it's a very common thing in the speaking and training industry.

One of them is the myth about learning styles or 'VAK' as it is sometimes known.

People talk about this theory like it is a scientific fact, that people are either:

Visual learners,

Auditory learners

or

Kinaesthetic learners.

Actually, when you look into that piece of research there is very little evidence that people are just visual, audio, or kinaesthetic learners because when I learn I am definitely a visual person because I love slides and images, I love looking at photographs etc. But, I also listen to audio books and podcasts in my car when I am travelling. Plus I also like to learn by doing as well!

So I am a **V**isual, **A**uditory AND **K**inaesthetic learner, which kind of ruins the theory.

So be careful that you don't just say stuff that you once heard, even from your boss!

It is so important to do proper research because as soon as you say something that isn't true or a handful of people in the audience think that you may have made it up they will be on their phones googling whether it's true or not. Therefore you have lost the audience for a while and unfortunately you can lose credibility too. I am not saying that 100% of the things that I have said in my many hours on stages are 100% true because things change, technology changes and people change too. New research comes out, so yes I have made some mistakes along the way, but more and more now I realise that the audience is Googling what I say as I speak so don't just say something without checking it out, unless it is deliberately for comedic effect, with a wink and smile.

To coin a new phrase – treat everything as 'fake news' unless you really look into it and find out the truth.

A great way of doing that is to Google it of course and Dr. John B Molidor, the former President of the National Speakers Association in the U.S. says that the easiest way of doing that is to Google the thing you are trying to research – type in that 'phrase' and afterwards type 'myth' or 'fact check'.

Do it that way so when you see the item you're interested in you will find the myth busting too. Snopes.com is a great website for this.

Have you seen the story about the wolf pack and the older wolves on social media? It was everywhere. The story goes that they put the older wolves at the front of the pack as they roam and they make sure that they are OK and they go at the pace of the older wolves. It's a wonderful story, it's a great picture but sadly it is not true. Wolves do show some of those signs but that isn't exactly what they do and so it's just become a nice internet story, meme and Facebook post. When I looked into it, I didn't find it to be true so I wouldn't use it in my talks. (Unless I am talking about myths or propagation because then maybe I would, like now.)

Do your research, it will serve you well, it will help you to go deeper into your subject but it will also give you credibility so people won't question what you say as much and it will help you to help them not to switch off from your talk. This is particularly true if your audience is made up of younger people who Google everything.

Let's do the world a service and fact-check all of our news to make sure it's not 'real' fake news!

Start your filing system today

It's always great to have a way of collecting research for a talk and one of the ways of doing that is to start your own basic filing system, this could be a box file, a drawer in your office, it could be an old fashioned folder that you can carry around. Basically it's somewhere you can collect everything you want to add about your particular subject.

I have several of these and I call them 'Tickle files'[3]. So, for instance if your focus is motivation like me, I have several 'motivation' 'tickle files' in my filing cabinet. It is simply things that 'tickle me' in some way, no more than that. Sometimes I make notes during the day, I collect articles or I scribble things down quickly, because if I don't write things down when I think about it – I forget. I have switched to electronic note taking now (more on that below), but sometimes when my phone is not available I will just scribble it onto a piece of paper and stick it in my pocket. When I first met speakers and comedians one of the things I realised is that they all carry notebooks and they simply write things down. We have got to carry a notebook with us, there is something about a physical notebook that works.

So start to collect things about your particular subject. There are two main reasons for this.

One, it gets everything into one place and **two** it gets you thinking more long term.

3. Steve McDermott an award winning speaker and a guy who helped me in the early days, he coined this phrase – I thought it was a great idea! I use it with his permission.

When you think longer term you will keep collecting anecdotes whenever anything grabs your attention. You see an article on a website? Take a snapshot of it and stick it in the tickle file. If you see something in the newspaper in a coffee shop take a photograph of it or rip the article out of the newspaper and stick it in your pocket (sorry Costa!), make sure you also add it to the tickle file.

When you are doing preparation you want some solid stuff that is timeless but also some up to date things as well, so when you are making a point you can say "Did you see this in the news last week?" and then bring out that piece of paper. Or you could have a picture of the newspaper on a slide or the paper itself, hold it up and actually read from the paper. I find that audiences quite like people reading stuff out because it looks good that we have done our research for that moment. Reading from a newspaper is ok on stage as long as you are only doing that for a few seconds then that's perfect – it's a little prop in a way.

Gather your information thoroughly then when you start to get the shape of your talk sorted, it means that you'll never panic as you have loads of information to draw on.

Online tickle file!

Evernote is your friend (other online note taking apps are available too – just make sure that they sync well and backup too!)

We can do all of these things electronically now of course, just grab things on your camera or in note form and Evernote will synchronise with all your devices. At its basic level it's free, so there are plenty of options – the main thing is to just capture your ideas.

Do your research thoroughly so that when you do have a talk you are not just there with a blank piece of paper or a blank white board. With the resources you have collated you can compile your talk more easily. Here is a photograph of some of my resources, the physical 'Tickle files' for motivation, education work, motivation for workplace, slides presentation skills, or just things that I think are interesting…

Find a way of capturing your ideas so you are not going back to the same old slides or presentations you compiled 10 years ago, or having to resort to stealing someone else's stuff! Build your own library, use your own stories but always remember to write them down so you have them to hand.

I was on holiday earlier this year and I overheard a woman sitting in the villa next to ours say this to her family. "All women are bitches because men make them like that!". I could hear her as plain as day, I was just there with my mouth open thinking, does she really think that? Wow! So, I grabbed a piece of paper, wrote it down and thought – I am going to use that sometime, and now I have! If you don't write it down – the things that you see, the people that you meet and the things that they say will literally be forgotten.

Write it down, grab a notebook, buy a Moleskine notebook for £15 or get to the Pound shop, (I am not an expert but I am guessing it will cost you about a pound).

Every presentation has a timeline:

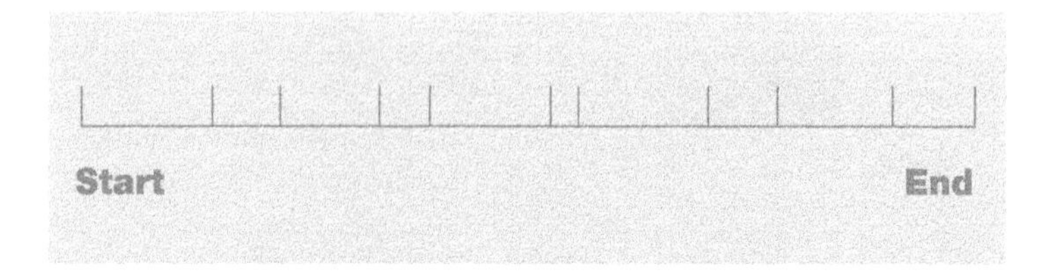

As well as having a start and end point, your presentation should also have some moments of change, interest and even intrigue. We don't speak in normal life in a monotone way without changes and points of interest and neither should your talk be 'flat'.

As you plan things think about the ways you can make changes to focus to keep the audience engaged. What are the peak points of interest you know will work? It might be a story, a video clip or a key moment, even just a pause when the audience can stop and think and take in what you've said.

Plan with the audience's attention span in mind and you are far less likely to ever deliver a dull talk again.

Develop over time the moments that you know work as key points on your presentations timeline. Like an experienced DJ always has a few tried and tested tunes that they know work when things have fallen a bit flat, we need those too as speakers to create the timeline of a more engaging talk.

Now we have learnt how to capture ideas we can start to write a talk…

Start with a blank page

All my note-books are blank, none of them have lines in them, I never use lined paper, and even if I'm ever given a nice embossed event or corporate notebook they mostly they come with lines on the pages so I end up giving them away.

Lined notebooks are the enemy of my creativity.

The problem with a lined notebook is if you are trying to plan a talk on one, whenever you use something with lines your brain ends up starting to put things into a running order. So what happens is, as you write four or five things down on a lined piece of paper your brain starts to worry about the order that you are putting things in, so your

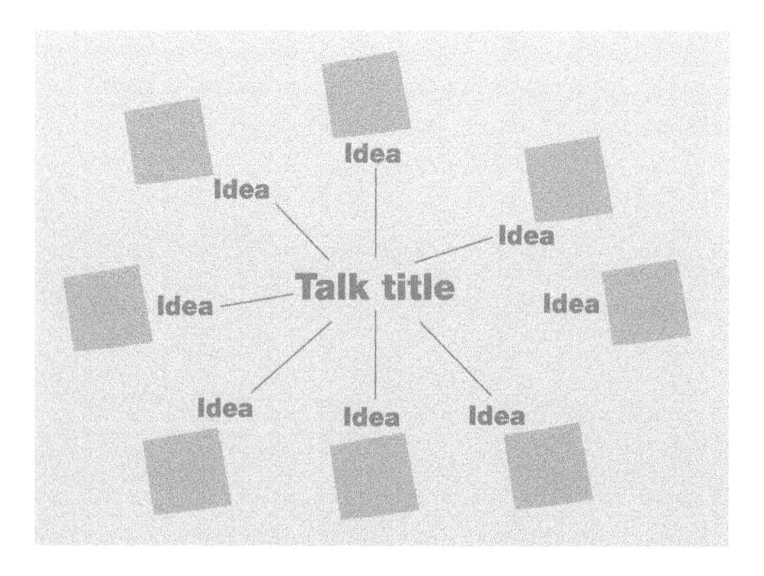

brain start to think "oh no I will put that second" and "I will put that third" and as you start to do that – the creative process stops because you become more bothered about the order of things than the creative process of capturing chunks or ideas that you need. So give away your lined notebooks and only buy blank notebooks in future. Or start to plan your talk on a whiteboard or on a flip chart paper.

To start, write the title in the middle, you don't have to do a complicated mind map or anything like that – you literally put the title in the middle, and then put a little line and write your first idea down, for instance intro, story, video clip, stats and just start building it up.

The key thing here is to take your time, unless you're panicking and your talk is tomorrow morning! You are better planning something weeks ahead if you have the chance, because your brain subconsciously starts to plan it and will do the work for you, reducing your stress and that panicked thought of "oh no I must do this now – I have got to have an idea, **I have got to have an idea!**"

I might find out that I am doing a talk in three months' time and start to plan it three months ahead, not because I have too much time on my hands but just because I have learned that when you plan ahead your brain does the work for you. So, you put your main details on the planning sheet and have a bit of a go. Maybe spend an hour pulling something together and then just leave it, take a photograph of it if you have to wipe it off the whiteboard or even better you might want to get an A3 notebook and then with a full piece of A3 paper you can start to plan it and then you can just fold it up into A4 and pop it in to your bag and it's easy to take with you.

The key thing here is to allow the idea to marinate. My favourite food in the world is Persian food, it's amazing, beautiful fluffy rice with berries, seeds and kebabs. Not the kebabs that look like a dodgy elephant's leg, like you often get, those are terrible. These are the ones done individually in a clay oven. But even more importantly the kebab meat is fantastic and the taste is out of this world. The reason why is because they marinate the meat. So, they might leave the meat overnight in spices and herbs, they marinate it so that it has this soft texture and an amazing taste to it. It is hard to beat.

That's what you want to do with your ideas for a talk, allow things to marinate, don't be in a rush. A new idea is just that, a new idea, it might not be the best, just because it's new doesn't mean that it's good. Ask Clive Sinclair or the inventor of 3D TV – whatever happened to that? Does everyone now sit in their living rooms every night with 3D glasses on? No! It was gimmick, a bad idea that was not going to work.

Allow your ideas to marinate over time and you will find that you are perhaps having a shower and all of a sudden an idea will pop into your mind, or maybe you are walking down the street and "Ah right I remember that" so you find a way of writing it down and get it onto the sheet or whiteboard. I have even heard of people having notepads in their shower, you can buy waterproof notepads! Write the idea down somehow and get it onto your planning sheet and when you do that you will find your talk will build up over time. Plan in your diary, maybe a couple of weeks before the talk, go through and start doing your planning fully, by then you will have built up loads of quality ideas, probably way too much. Too much info is a good way to start, it means that you have got ideas that you can work from. You have a solid base and foundation to work from and that can make a real difference. Planning with lots of time is the ideal scenario.

On my resources page is a quick planning sheet too – **http://bit.ly/GetGoodPresExtras**

Post-it!

The next stage is now to make your information and planning more flexible, the easy solution?

Use Post-it notes.[4]

Every little chunk of information you now have on your sheet just make them into a single Post-it note.

Every idea needs to become one Post-it note.

Don't use a normal pen though, use a Sharpie or marker pen because at this stage we don't want too much detail.

Detail will come later on in your deeper research and rehearsal, what you need at the moment is the main ideas, followed by two or three little things that you will make a further point about.

4. Many people use a technique similar to this and I'm not saying that it is original to me in any way, is anything original? But, I am grateful for the time that fellow PSA speaker Alan Stevens took to explain this to me many years ago.

So you might have fifteen Post-it notes all with different things on them.

The great thing about Post-it notes of course is not only are they cheap and available at your Pound shop (which will cost approximately a pound as you know!) but also that they are movable. There is also a free phone/tablet app that digitises them too.

Now we can start to make the running order of your talk come to life. Remember, first these were on a blank piece of paper and now they are on Post-it notes, so we haven't got anything into any order just yet.

What you do now with the Post-it notes is stick them onto a wall or whiteboard, or your A3 paper and start to put them into some rough order.

What do you think should be first?

What should you talk about first?

What should you talk about last?

Start there and think "Ah that would fit here best" and "if I mention this at that point it would be great" and "if I mention this, then that would be..."

Start to build up your presentation. Of course these are still moveable so you might decide to change them around as your talk develops and you start to "see your presentation come to life".

So, even now nothing is in a final order and we haven't touched any

PowerPoint slides yet either, we are still in a creative phase. So, use the Post-it notes and keep that flexibility to change. The beauty of this technique is that you can thin things out too, because you have probably got too much information.

Most of the clients I work with I reckon they can easily get rid of a third or more of their content.

Yes, you read that right!

When they come to me with their talk, they are often speaking way too fast and simply have too much content, too much information and too many bullet points (I think some days that even two bullet points is too many). Most are going to overrun on their allotted time. With the Post-it note technique you have the ability to thin out your talk easily.

The great thing is that you have built up, say, an hours' worth of information, and then you turn up at the venue or you might get a phone call the day before and the organiser tells you that you only have 40 minutes now.

Now at this point you can panic thinking "oh no" because if you get less time you only have two options. One, you speak faster so it becomes really boring and you become like a machine gun speaker or, two you remove some content. When you remove content it becomes your talk more and has a bit of breathing space, time for gestures and pauses, it dramatically changes the way that you deliver.

This is all because we have got it on Post-it notes and blank paper and we haven't got anything in any order.

The technique above can revolutionise the way that you prepare and deliver a presentation.

From now on, think in chunks and Post-it notes of information not a whole talk.

Because talks are often just chunks of 'stuff' linked together well.

You need to resist the temptation to go to your slides to do what you have always done.

Chunks!

Plan in an open and creative way like this and you will start to see your talk not as a whole thing because that can bring anxiety, but as little chunks of information. I have never delivered the same talk twice, yes sure I have in one way, but on the whole what I have is a bagful of 'chunks' that I know help people and when my client wants a certain focus I just pick and choose the correct chunks. I might choose a little bit of this chunk and a little bit of that chunk and I might use a bit out of another talk that I have done too. So I simply use my 'Tickle files' and 'chunks' to build a bespoke speech. That's how I tend to write things now, I might add new 'chunks' often but still I choose the chunks instead of writing a whole new talk every time.

There are of course many other ways to plan a talk, the main thing is that you allow the creativity to flow and find a way that works best for you. I think that the method I have just told you about will be revolutionary for many and time saving too. If you want to use other techniques then please do let me know what works for you. Most of the professional speakers that I know here in the UK and Ireland will use something like this technique. A way of working where grabbing chunks of information, structuring them and then practicing your talk in the best way that suits you is always going to win.

Most talks given aren't word perfect and they aren't scripted but they are directed in the way that I have explained to you.

When you are preparing, many say that you should have your best line at the end and your second-best line at the beginning but always 'top and tail well'. Think about what is going to be your opener not just "hello" or introduce your company name, and then do your company history – everyone does that.

Can you deliver a challenge and then fill in the middle bits, that's a great way to give a good talk. Keep it flexible, keep it fluid and you will find that your creativity really comes to the fore.

We are all creatives, we are all here on earth to be creative people, it's just finding a way of getting our brains to do that well – we are all different. But I can say that if you spend your whole time with lined paper only, you may be restricting your creativity, you have to allow the space to let your brain do the work.

So now you can prepare well to deliver a great talk. Let's work on delivery…

Space for your notes

Delivery

How to Get Good when you are on your feet, in front of an audience

Here's a few things that I have found to be really useful. Firstly, learn how to start well, this is not just an opening line. Find a way that brings energy to the room. Find a way of starting to differentiate you from the previous speaker.

Get people off their phones and 'into the room'.

That's what we are battling with, getting people off their phones and stopping them thinking about what they are having for dinner!

Using something that grabs people's attention is key.

There are several ways to do this, use the one that fits your personality best. I tend to go for a big hello and then some kind of statement that grabs people's attention. Even in a keynote I will get people to laugh, use an ice-breaker or a bit of humour, something that breaks the pattern of what's gone before. You could start with a statement which says something that they weren't expecting. You could use a key statement like

"Have you ever thought…?"

"Are you like me…."

"In 1929 in San Antonio, Texas…"

If you want to see a great speech intro I suggest having a look at Mohammed Qahtani who won the Toastmasters World championship in 2015. The intro to his talk 'The Power of Words' is great.

The context of his talk is key. He talks about smoking and there is an audible gasp from the audience as he looks like he is lighting up a cigarette, no one ever does that on stage because in certain states in America it's worse than in the UK, people just do not smoke in public anymore.

The audible gasp gets people off their phones and gets people listening to him, he grabs the first prize and wins the Toastmasters World Speaking Championship.

Can you remember any intros from any presentations that you have seen? A good one is very memorable.

The video is on YouTube or my book webpage here: http://bit.ly/GetGoodPresExtras

Like Mohammed, try to do anything apart from saying your name and you are glad to be there, it's an honour etc.

I often get people to put their hands up for a few questions early on, it's a style and technique that I have developed and works well for me, because when people put their hands up they are engaged. They stop chatting to each other and engage. I have made jokes before where I have said "put your hands up if you are here". I wait to see how many people actually hear me, then I will say "OK, put your hands up if you're not here". "Why don't you give the person next to you a nudge to check if they are awake?" Something like that will break the ice and then I can start with my presentation and I can start delivering what I have planned. A statement that might shock them can work well (be careful though!), or just gently tell them something about yourself.

Find your style, try things out.

Written introductions for event MCs and hosts

The best way to start the whole thing off though is to have a written introduction for the event host or MC. Most professionals use well-thought brief written introductions, particularly in a business environment where it's a little more structured.

People will usually introduce you anyway so it's better to give them something that you want them to say rather than something that they randomly came up with. You want something that sets you up with your credibility but without making you sound pompous or like someone who is trying too hard.

A few lines of introduction can save you time, then you don't have to brag and tell them your qualifications and work history, but it allows you to hit the ground running. Some people seem to need to wind up at the beginning of their talk so a good intro will help us to leap straight in there and make an impact. We should start warming up when we are off stage, not on stage, that's a waste of time.

Don't just think about what you are going to say – think about a written introduction that sits well with you.

Here is a little guide for writing your own from writer, broadcaster and speaker Jeremy Nicholas[5]:

You need three paragraphs, or better still, three lines.

1. Who you are – You need to say who you are, but without giving

5. Used with his kind permission

your name. It should intrigue us. We should be thinking this sounds like a very qualified person. We're so lucky that we're here today to hear this wonderful person. Who can it be?

2. What you are going to talk about – Tell us what's going to be in the talk. It might be the title of the talk or the information that you are going to give us. It might be what we'll be able to do differently after hearing the talk. It should be something that makes us sit and want to listen. It should not tell us the duration of the talk. When I hear our next speaker is going to talk for about an hour, my heart sinks.

3. Why you are the person to listen to on this subject – This is the bit where you can really show-off. Don't worry, someone else will be reading it out, so you can really go to town. This is where you say 'just back from speaking in Cape Town' or 'just wowed them at the IBM conference' or 'award winning broadcaster'.

It should be short and punchy and should give the audience something to look forward to and something to worry or wonder about. The emphasis should not be on you, but how you are going to benefit the audience. And the very last thing that the emcee should say is your name

Here is Jeremy's intro:

Our next speaker is an award-winning TV and radio broadcaster. He shares with corporate and professional speakers the skills he's picked up in thirty years on-air.

Today he's going to show how you can use humour in your business presentations, to ensure your audience is engaged and entertained for your whole talk.

It's a talk that won him the coveted Professional Speaking Award of Excellence and has seen him speak to audiences in South London, Southampton and South Africa.

Please welcome Jeremy Nicholas.

Tailor your intro to the audience

There are probably lots of things that you could include about yourself in your intro, but try and bear in mind the audience and why you've been invited. Use the key points that fit best with that audience. Here's some about Jeremy:

- Sixteen years as the stadium announcer at West Ham United. (Great when I'm speaking in East London and Essex, but not a great intro in the north of England.)
- Broadcaster who won the New York Radio Academy Award for his live commentary on the Hillsborough Disaster for BBC Radio. (It adds gravitas for business events, but not for after- dinner talks.)
- Lost out to Anthea Turner in the hunt for a new Blue Peter presenter. (Not great for business talks, but good for after-dinner.)
- 42nd person in the UK to be made a Fellow of the PSA. (Good for all corporate audiences.)
- Met his wife on match dot com. (Ideal for networking events.)

- Voice of the global best selling FIFA video games. (Great for schools)

N.B. If your name is difficult to spell or pronounce, feel free to put a note at the top about that including a phonetic spelling if needed. I know many speakers who have been introduced wrongly due to difficult spellings or pronunciations, and you don't want your first line to be "No, that's not me!".

In the appendix are a few real introductions used by other Pro speakers too.

Press Pause

> "The right word may be effective but no word was ever as effective as a rightly timed pause."
>
> **Mark Twain**

There is nothing worse than someone who speaks at a hundred miles an hour always trying to get as much out as they possibly can without taking a pause. As an audience member it's stressful to watch them.

I am quite a fast speaker, but I have learned over the years to add pauses, that's why I use props, it's why I drink water, it's why I use big slides and videos too. These are all ways of pausing my talk so people can take it in. I was coaching someone the other day and they spoke very fast. They often gave out brilliant nuggets of wisdom, but because they flew past them, no-one heard them. They were wasting their wisdom, throwing it away to be trodden underfoot. I got them to slow down and it changed everything, including their enjoyment of their own presentation.

If you are making a good point or your main point – something you really want to get over well, it's so important to bring that with a slowed down delivery, then people will understand it. If you speak really quickly all the time it becomes like white noise to an audience. So, learn to pace yourself and learn to pause.

Margaret Thatcher the former U.K. Prime Minister was brilliant at pausing. According to her colleagues, she had no discernible sense of humour and was not a particularly likeable speaker, but she was the queen of pauses, pauses that made, I think, what she said much more digestible and memorable. Her most famous speech was probably "The lady's not for turning", and in it she made a joke that her speech writers gave her which she delivered deadpan and used a massive pause, I have timed the pause on this speech which was 12 seconds. She was willing to pause for applause and laughter and just wait and wait and wait, 12 seconds in all before she hit her final line "The Lady's not for Turning".

12 seconds on stage without speaking must have felt like an eon.

(These videos are on the book resources webpage here – http://bit.ly/GetGoodPresExtras)

Martin Luther King Jnr was also great at pausing and as I said he almost sang when he presented but he knew that he could exteeeeeend his vowels and exteeeeeend his woooooords to make a point, to invent a pause so that he wasn't delivering at a hundred miles an hour. Genius.

Bear in mind though we are looking for a natural pause here NOT a hammed up thespian Shakespearean pause for dramatic effect. Eugh! It has to be natural and it has to be believable, otherwise you risk putting a barrier up between you and your audience. Try it out.

Pace, pause and tone

With pace, it's about learning to speed up and slow down; with pauses it's literally about stopping. The problem with pausing is that we have adrenaline running through our veins while we are speaking, (everyone has adrenaline while they are speaking, it is basically fight or flight so our whole system is speeded up). So you might pause for what you think is 3 or 4 seconds when actually it's a one tenth of a second. It's a tiny pause and the audience doesn't notice it, so any of us, including me, have to learn to physically pause.

Drinking water is a great technique to use. If you know that you are a fast speaker like me, taking a drink of water mid-flow works well. Taking a sip of water is a great way for you to pause and for the audience to take a breath.

Pausing in your delivery is good, but add a change of pace and tone too.

Dull speakers speak with the same tone and volume of their voice often for the whole presentation, you may remember someone who has done this. It is an engagement killer. Sometimes it's nerves, sometimes it's just the fact that they haven't had any feedback to help them with this.

The solution is simple.

Make sure that you are naturally changing your tone of voice as and when it is required in your presentation.

The volume of, and tone of your voice are part and parcel of your presentation.

Don't change it in a false way, but an honest way so you speak quieter for certain parts and louder for others. Stories are great for this, they can change the tone of your voice easily, little asides and looks at the audience can change your tone of voice too. It is change that makes the difference. Standing behind a lectern doesn't help at all (it never does to be honest – I hate them). Doing parts of your talk from specific areas of the stage is what people do to adjust this simply. So, if I am on the left-hand side of the stage I can become a little quieter and if I am on the right-hand side of the stage I can become bigger and louder – whatever you need to do to remind yourself, do it.

The same tone and volume the whole time will put people to sleep or make them check Facebook. I'm naturally fairly loud and can command a room but I've learnt to be quieter too when delivering, give it a go.

I often think that primary school teachers are good at this, in an assembly they often get slower and quieter the more primary school kids that are in front of them. They realise that there is no point shouting or being louder than the kids, so they say "shhhhhssss", then establish eye contact and sometimes even crouch down as they go quieter and slower, until the whole of the school is looking at them. Then they deliver sometimes in a whispered tone, and they get heard. Brilliant.

When you need people to *really* listen, learn to pause, and change the pace and tone of your delivery too.

Voice volume

If you are too loud, it is uncomfortable for the audience, if you are too quiet they'll miss key content, and if you are monotone they'll tune out.

One of the things that people get bad feedback for in my sessions is that people simply can't hear them and that's generally because people speak up front using their normal conversational voice. If you are doing a presentation you have to raise your voice slightly. You don't need to shout but you do need to raise your volume so that people can hear what you are saying on the back row.

An easy tip to do this well is simply to speak to the back row not the front row. When you are presenting you need to project your voice to the back of the room.

Don't take the bad advice out there and stare and speak to the clock on the back wall of the room because you want to avoid the eye contact. Get eye contact with the back row and that will naturally make you raise your voice as you lift your head a bit and your chest will be lifted up too. The process of lifting your head can just be enough for you to project your voice loud enough. It is easy to do.

I do some exercises around this when I am training. Basically imagine there was a conversation taking place in a room and you want to be loud enough to be heard by everyone on the other side of the room but without shouting. Shouting is obviously aggressive and you don't want that. So, find a way of raising your voice by lifting your head and your chin and being more confident in your voice. You do need to get people's attention and raising the volume of your voice is one of the key ways of doing this.

Don't let your good material get lost because your voice is not loud enough.

Mr. Brent

In 2001 the world was introduced to a TV character called David Brent who was in the UK version of 'The Office' which has gone on to be a big show in the US as well. He only did two series and a couple of specials here in the UK. When the first episode aired, people thought it was a real documentary. What was funny and painful about the series was that David Brent thought that he was very successful and a great speaker and so he did a few presentations during the series. The most painful of these was his "motivational talk" that he did to a small group of people in a dull small conference room. You can see it here too: http://bit.ly/GetGoodPresExtras

Not only is it funny it's also kind of sad because it's very close to home for people like myself who speak for a living. When you dissect the talk, you will see that really what he is doing wrong is just not understanding his audience. It looks like he does everything a speaker coach might tell you to do, he tells a story, he uses a famous quote, he does all sorts of things but it's just a bit too much and he comes across as putting down and belittling the audience.

Engaging an audience, without seeming to talk down to them or make them feel awkward like Brent does, is a really subtle art.

Sure he might be speaking but actually his misses them by a mile.

Have a look at the clip. What do you think he does wrong? Be specific.

What is his main problem and why is that?

If he is so cringe-worthy and bad then what can we do to not be like him? Specifically what can we do when we are speaking so we don't end up having 'David Brent-isms?'

I think fundamentally it is about connection, when you know your audience and you know they are a group of human beings you can make connections to them. David Brent doesn't do that, what he does is inflict his talk on his audience, he manages to not care who they are, what their reactions are, what their background is or why they are there, but he forces his stuff on them.

The last thing you want to do as a speaker is be cringe-worthy.

Don't be David Brent.

Don't just talk

The words that we use, our body language, our pace, our pause, our smile, our eye contact and engagement with the audience are all important for one simple reason.

The reason is that, put simply: **talking isn't necessarily good communication**.

Many times I have sent emails to people, I have written something on Social Media and it's been misinterpreted or misunderstood, I am sure you have had the same thing. Even when we write things down it can be misinterpreted so easily and when we just talk, that also is not necessarily good communication, it can be misinterpreted, it can just not work.

Filters

There are a thousand filters between the words that we say and the brains of our audience.

"I will tell them something and therefore they will have received everything that I told them". Of course that's not how it works. It is naive to think so.

We can be shouted at but if someone is smiling we don't take it seriously.

We can receive lovely encouraging words from people but if they say it in an angry voice we don't hear it.

You can try that sometime, you can tell the dog it is being naughty but do it in a nice voice and of course it doesn't understand you – because talking is not necessarily good communication.

If you want to be a great presenter you have to immediately stop thinking that everything that you say is received by your audience. In between you and the audience there are all those filters of culture, background, religion, what they have done today, what their family members have told them, what social media has being saying to them, what their friends have said on Snapchat, Instagram or WhatsApp before they get to your event. All of this is bombarding your audience's heads and so just talking is not necessarily going to get through to them.

We have to engage in many different ways to get through the filters. So, presenting an engaging speech is not just about talking. There is so much more to learn in order to engage and get our message across.

So from now on think **"Is what I'm saying getting through here?"** not "Am I telling them the right stuff?"

"it's really hard for a blunt instrument to understand but arrogance and self-awareness seldom go hand in hand".

'M' in the Bond film Casino Royale

Authentic

"Of undisputed origin or authorship, genuine."

"Accurate in representation of the facts, trustworthy, reliable."

Those are dictionary definitions of authentic.

I believe the best speakers are the ones who are truly authentic.

A client approached me a couple of years ago, they had obviously read my website and heard that I was a "Motivational Speaker" so they gave me a call. I often speak to clients on the phone as soon as I can because it really helps, I am a speaker after all and I find it a much better way than email to communicate. After I had spoken to them for a couple of minutes they suddenly stopped me and said "oh you're really nice". I reflected on that and I thought why did they think that I wouldn't be nice? I guess it's the job title, I guess they thought I was arrogant, that maybe all professional speakers are full of themselves, I guess they thought that I wouldn't be authentic, I wouldn't be me. It always struck me as funny that they thought that I was ok to chat to! We have got to be ourselves when we are speaking we can't be anybody else, we shouldn't pretend to be anyone else, even someone you respect or has mentored you.

Someone once said to me "The stage is a very dangerous place, unless we are actually called to be there". Unless we have authenticity and integrity I think that this is right, because the stage brings out our real self in the little things that we say, the little asides, the little looks we give. People can read us quite well and if we are different off stage than we are on stage then that's very noticeable. I believe that I try to be, as best I can, the same on and off stage. Except that when I am on stage I should be a little bit more interesting than off stage, because I am performing a little bit and telling my funniest stories.

So, authenticity and integrity are two of the legs that a speaker should stand on, you can't be a disorganised productivity expert, or a customer service expert speaker who treats their customers badly. You have to be the real deal and we have to speak about what we know and what we live. Don't tell people you have done stuff if you haven't, let them see the real you. I believe that professional speakers' reputations can be poor, because of bad experiences in the past. Their credibility can be low because people think they are full of themselves, but when other speakers have lost it for us because of their bad behaviour and their short term attitude of profit before engaging the audience, we have to go in the opposite direction. We have got to be authentic and be ourselves. We should tell people that you can be a speaker and be a good person and be the real deal. I think being good is free and doesn't cost us anything. We do have to challenge our audiences of course but we should never pretend that we are something we are not. I think that's what I have seen often. People pretending that they are more successful than they are and saying that they have done more work than they have. We have got to decide to become completely authentic both on and off the stage, and when we occasionally fail, just admit it, learn from it, take it in your stride and try again. I make mistakes all the time.

An authentic speaker is someone who speaks about what they know and is comfortable in their own skin.

I will be writing a book about authenticity next as I continue to research and speak around this subject, so I won't give you the full thing here and now. My encouragement to you as a speaker, whether pro or amateur is really just to try and be yourself. You don't have to pretend to be anyone else, you don't have to be a person hiding behind a posh suit, you don't have to wear a certain brand of clothing, or a certain brand of shoes to make you who you are. People ultimately want to connect with real people when they are listening to speakers. Be yourself.

We are human beings not information delivering robots

Showing your little flaws and foibles here and there is endearing, not off-putting to an audience, no matter who they are. Letting people know that you are not perfect is a strength not a weakness. That's why I love the film 'Wall-E' because it shows a robot with flaws, foibles and a heart. You are not there just to deliver what your boss says you have to deliver. The best way for you to deliver something is to deliver it as you, in your own skin because that's the person that you really are and that's who you should be on the stage.

Do everything you can to make your delivery great, but above all be yourself and learn to become more and more comfortable in your own skin.

Once you are, you will find that your feedback ratings go up and you will feel more comfortable presenting. And then the unthinkable may happen – you will start to look forward to presenting rather that dreading it like most people do.

Learning to be yourself is a process not an instant fix, you're not a Pot Noodle.

5 quick ways to be yourself when presenting:

1. Tell stories that happened to you.
2. Don't pretend that you are perfect.
3. Ask for feedback and watch video back to make your body language more open.
4. Smile more.
5. Be kind to yourself, before, during and afterwards too. Getting your talk ever so slightly wrong is not the end of the world.

"What you are…thunders
so that I cannot hear what you say…"

Ralph Waldon Emmerson

Humour

People ask me a lot about humour.

My feedback usually says that I'm quite a funny speaker, at least I've learned to be over time. As you may realise I am a comedy geek too, I have done stand-up comedy and I love making people laugh, it's one of the things that I really enjoy about my work as a speaker. There are a lot of different views of humour, different styles that people use too. I tried to 'tell jokes' for a while. One of my favourite comedians is Tim Vine, he does puns and short punchy one-liners, I have tried that style before and it just didn't really suit me. It's not what I do now. I might use an occasional pun here and there, but it's not really who I am. I have discovered that with humour the easiest and safest humour you can ever use, particularly in the culture that I am in here in the UK is self-deprecating humour.

I never have a go at my audience like a comedian might do, I never have a go at my clients (obviously!), but I will always have a little go at myself. I am not having a self-esteem crisis or anything, it just works well. i.e. someone said to me at an event once "you really look like Keith Chegwin!" (Keith Chegwin was a 1980's British TV presenter who is known now for Celebrity Big Brother and other random celebrity stunts). As they said it I realised yes maybe I do look a bit like Keith – so now, quite early on in most of my talks, I mention it. What's funny about that is that anyone over the age of 40 will understand the joke and those under 40 don't know who Keith Chegwin is, so I even use that and say of course if you're old enough you will understand this and if you don't you ask one of the old people, so that gets a second laugh about it. People say "oh yes, I see it now, I thought I recognised you" and so it mentions an elephant in the room and gets a laugh too – in the process they know that I don't take myself too seriously either – so that little gag does several things to help me engage an audience.

Your aim for humour in speeches is to aim for a smile and not a belly laugh. And do not tell jokes! Jokes usually divide an audience, good humour brings them together.

Don't go with the expectation of being Jerry Seinfeld, Peter Kay, or Billy Connolly, you won't get people rolling in the aisles, thinking that you are funniest person that they have ever heard, just aim for a smile. Aim for something that will help them say "this person seems normal and relaxed, they don't take themselves too seriously.

On my resources webpage http://bit.ly/GetGoodPresExtras are some more ways that you can inject humour into your talks written by the U.S. comedian and speaker Karen Eddington[6].

You may think that you are not funny at all. I understand that. But remember that humour can be added to a talk just like better content and stories. Ask someone about it, 'get some help, try out some humour and find your style.

Bill Gove the former National Speakers Association's President in the U.S. was once asked whether you have to be funny to be a professional speaker. He said "Only if you want to get paid."[7]

6. Used with her kind permission
7. Quoted in 'How To Win Your Audience With Bombproof Humor...' By Karl Righter

The same applies to any speaker. "Do you have to be funny to be a speaker?" "No, but if you want to be a good one, you do." Not using humour in a talk is like playing the piano with only the white keys. Sure, it is possible but why restrict your options? Presentations are better with natural, appropriate humour.

The subtlety of challenge

Challenge is key, but confrontation is (99.9% of the time) a no-no.

There is a very fine line between challenge and confrontation.

As speakers, we should be challenging the norm but we should be approachable in our delivery. If we don't challenge as a speaker they might as well invite a roll of wallpaper to events – we are often there to challenge people's mind-sets, to challenge the way organisations work, the way that someone spends their life, but we don't have to confront people. Confrontation is very different – it's aggressive, it is "you need to do that" using the word 'you' is more confrontational than using the word 'we' or 'us' for instance.

It is the difference between "You need to do this" or "Why don't we try this?".

"What if we started thinking about life differently?", is a very different phrase to "I think you should think about your life differently!".

I don't think we are paid or invited to confront people unless they are specifically asking for that. I think it's always better to challenge people and include ourselves in the challenge. Even if you have gone further than they have, or you have achieved whatever the goal is that you are talking about, I still think that we should include ourselves as it makes the talk more inclusive, and the challenge deeper because they realise that the speaker is being authentic, not aggressive.

Everyone in the world suffers from procrastination so if we say that we have beaten it, that is nonsense because we haven't, everyone still suffers from it.

So, if you say something like "wouldn't it be great if we could beat procrastination. Here's a few things that I have learnt about it. Here's no 1, no 2, no 3. The main thing I found is that…".

That is so different from "**I** am an expert in procrastination **I** have solved it completely and here are **my** top 3 tips that you should learn today! (Adopt 'power pose' at this point!)".

"I" is the 18th most popular word spoken in English[8]. We as speakers must use it very sparingly.

In U.K. culture that really puts people off and they start to think "I am not listening to this idiot. I am not going to listen to them because they have confronted me and only seem to speak about themselves."

So, challenge at times, but don't confront, unless you are a boxer at their weigh-in.

8. "The 500 Most Commonly Used Words in the English Language" Based on the combined results of British English, American English and Australian English surveys of contemporary sources in English: newspapers, magazines, books, TV, radio and real life conversations – the language as it is written and spoken today. http://www.world-english.org/english500.htm

Using and Presenting Data – How to Crunch numbers!

Complex and intense graphs, diagrams and data tables often don't interest anyone when we are presenting because no-one can see data if it's poorly presented. Your audience may want to analyse the full data afterwards and that's fine – you can of course give them a hand-out in person (only ever give a hand-out after you've spoken) or online using a link to one of the dozens of cloud options available like Dropbox, iCloud, Google Drive etc, just like I've done with the book resources webpage.

But as JesseDee on SlideShare points out it's up to us to crunch the numbers for them before the presentation. Clear communication is our goal, so pull out the key bits of data and present them clearly, the rest is just background noise.

Background noise doesn't help your message stick, clarity does.

Be disciplined here and your data (if you use it) will shine to back up your message not descend on the room like a bank of fog clouding your audience's ability to see the point you're making. Data doesn't have to be dull. If your data is key then why not get someone to make it look good? Jared Fanning[9] took the data from https://hubpages.com/literature/mostreadbooks and brilliantly created the info-graphic overleaf.

9. jaredfanning.com – used with kind permission

TOP 10
MOST READ BOOKS
IN THE WORLD
Based on number of books printed and sold over the last 50 years. Some titles may have had more copies printed than some of these books, but a vast number of those books were not sold, so we'll assume that they did not get read.
820
400
103
65
57
43
33
30
27
THE HOLY BIBLE
QUOTATIONS FROM CHAIRMAN MAO TSE-TUNG
Harry Potter
J.K. ROWLING
THE LORD OF THE RINGS
J.R.R. TOLKIEN
THE ALCHEMIST
PAULO COELHO
THE DA VINCI CODE
DAN BROWN
The twilight saga
STEPHENIE MEYER
GONE WITH THE WIND
MARGARET MITCHELL
THINK AND GROW RICH
NAPOLEON HILL
THE DIARY OF ANNE FRANK
ANNE FRANK
JAREDFANNING.COM

'Show and Tell'

Do you remember in primary school doing 'show and tell'?

You take an item into school, maybe your favourite toy or even your pet and then do a little talk in front of the class? Maybe several of you got up and talked that day?

'Show and tell' is a great technique to use when you are speaking, it helps you to use props well too.

The 'Show'

Simply show something – act it out, explain it in great detail, hold it up, admire it and wax lyrically about your favourite beermat!

Maybe do this on the right hand side of the stage.

The 'Tell'

Then walk to another part of the stage and tell them what this means to you, your own story. Maybe the beermat reminds you of a great night out you had, old friends long gone or the time working behind a bar in your first ever job.

'The Show' is the object and 'The Tell' is about you.

It brings things alive, even old smelly beermats.

What could you 'show and tell' in your next presentation?

It was a Tuesday night in the spring of 1999, I'd had a long day but went to the school I worked in to do the Year 7 disco from 7 to 9 pm. I was pretty exhausted (with twin baby girls at home) and the last thing I wanted to do was load my car up with cds, speakers and equipment. So I arrived not exactly feeling full of joy!

But I went into the school hall and started to set things up for my standard two-hour cheesy party disco with 'The Macarena' and all the other classics. As a youth worker, I had learned to always get helpers. I wanted some of the young people to come and help with the DJ gear so I could hang out with them a bit, and one or two of them asked if they could DJ with me too.

A young-looking Year 7 lad (11 years old) came to help out. He was small, a bit scruffy looking and to be honest slightly unwashed too. He seemed about half the size of me. We chatted, laughed and he drank loads of Coke and ate endless Walkers salt and vinegar crisps. I allowed him to plan the music and put on some CDs and he really enjoyed getting involved. I was putting a CD on ready for the next track when he tapped me on the shoulder and said something which still stays with me today. I leant over to hear him clearly and he shouted in my ear, while spitting salt and vinegar Crisps at me, "I wish you were my brother."

It was one of those moments when I didn't know what to do. I had gone with a fairly bad attitude and didn't particularly want to be there, but 'John' was so happy just to be with me for the evening that he said those words to me.

I asked about him in school the next day and was told he had a very difficult time at home, and even though he wasn't doing well at school, they kept him there as much as possible (attached to one teacher most of the time) because they felt it was safer for him to be in school than it was for him to be at home. My just hanging out with him and letting him be a DJ's helper at a school disco made such a difference to him. When he said that he wished I was his brother, half of me wanted to burst into tears and the other half wanted to give him a big hug. It was a complete surprise and I didn't know how to react to it to be honest.

That night brought real focus and clarity to my role as a youth worker. One little comment from a Year 7 kid who smelled of salt and vinegar crisps affected my life and work for ever – far more than any facts and figures ever could.

That little interaction made me realise why I did my previous job and kept me going for a long time.

I have told that story a few times over the years. Once I told it as a brand new speaker in front of a group of Pros and one of them said to me "that was a great story – I want to work with you!" Now we do work together and my friend David Hyner still refers to this story and often throws bags of salt and vinegar crisps at me at awkward moments!

The Power of Story

If I could emphasise one thing away for you to take away from reading this book I think I would choose this.

Tell more stories

Less data, no death by PowerPoint.

Tell more stories

When I work and do my presentation skills courses I genuinely see people doing talks time and time again without using stories.

I don't mean just made up random abstract stories that don't go anywhere, but stories with a purpose, like the one you just heard. That was real, that was me, I tell that story sometimes when I am speaking to teachers and youth workers because it affected me and I know it has affected other people too. I have seen people tear up because they realise again "oh that's why I do my work".

A story is something that you remember, and it can go deep too.

So, pause now and think of all the talks you have been to – business talks, wedding talks, community groups, youth work, whatever your background is – of all the talks that you have heard in your life, which are the ones that you remember?

I am guessing you remember one where an unusual thing happened like someone fell off a chair or the stage or a story told stayed with you.

Stories make content "stickier".

So, if you have got great content and you are running a business helping your clients, tell your clients' stories. Or if you work for a charity and you are making a massive difference, tell the story of the difference that you have made.

It really isn't rocket surgery as someone famous once said!

Just tell your story, and tell it well.

Now obviously there is an art to storytelling but fundamentally people are interested in your story.

One of the most popular websites in recent years has been 'Humans of New York'. There is now a 'Humans' of every other city too, it is very popular. 'Humans of New York' took off because a guy called Brandon Stanton started a photography project with the aim of taking 10,000 pictures of New Yorkers. He started taking pictures and began chatting to the people that he had taken the pictures of, writing their stories and publishing them online. The photos are fantastic and show the quirky and interesting people that he captures. But what people really connected to was their stories, people would open up to him about abuse, drug addition, struggles at work, mental health issues or just funny things that have happened to them. That's what made that website so fantastic. Great photography, yes, but stories about real people.

People connect with people and that is what stories do, they make connections.

If you have the ability to do this, stop right now and write down some of the stories that you need to tell in your talks, maybe not soon but in the future. Ones that you have might have hidden away or forgotten. Remember, you can change the names of people and locations, there are ways of hiding sensitive information so you don't have to share everything. That lad isn't called 'John' that I told you about, because I wouldn't want to embarrass him if he ever read this book. I don't know where he is now but I wouldn't ever want to use his real name. Write down now all of the stories that you need to tell. Client stories, stories from your youth, funny things that happened to you on the bus or in the train station, or when boarding a plane.

What are YOUR stories? Start collecting them and put them in your Tickle File.

My rationale is simple.

If stories make your content stickier why wouldn't you want to use them?

According to Cognitive Psychologist Jerome Bruner, a fact that is wrapped in a story a makes it 22 times more likely to be remembered.

If your talk could be 22 times more memorable than the one that went before you, would you want that?

If you are pitching for £1m of business and you are one of 6 people that day, you need to be remembered.

It's as simple as that. You can be up to 22 times more memorable.

So don't shoot yourself in the foot and not use stories in your presentations.

Making your stories better

The simple way to make stories better is to act them out, be 'in the story' as you tell it – mention the sights, the smells, and how you felt at the time, this makes them much more powerful. Also it's good to strip any extra information away too, proper full names and information isn't that important. So saying "In the Spring of 1999" is much effective than saying "In 1999, I think it was a Tuesday, maybe the 8th of April , or was it the 9th of April? Mmmm, not sure – it was sunny though I think".

At my book resources page you can watch how one story has really made people stop and think. They simply told the stories of a few of the items in their shop.

Click here for more: http://bit.ly/GetGoodPresExtras

How to craft a story

I heard Mike Blissett talking about storytelling with information taken from his own life, with a bit of psychology and some common practice he says that the keys to a good story are in these 4 points:

Step 1 – It is a turning point.

(When John told me "I wish you were my brother")

Step 2 – It has significant people in it.

(John)

Step 3 – What did you learn then?

(I realised why I did my job)

Step 4 – Who are you today because of that moment?

(I am a more people focused person now, and someone who knows his calling)

Remember your stories, write them down, collect them, craft them, remove excess information and tell them well for more impact…

Richard's story

Richard McCann has spent many years telling his story about the day he found out that his mum had become a victim of someone who became known as the Yorkshire Ripper, a man called Peter Sutcliffe. He tells his amazing story with a lot of grace and humour. I was working with Richard one day and he told me another story too.

He was involved in 'The Forgiveness Project' working in prisons and difficult situations, talking about forgiveness, what that really means in someone's life and how we can change the situations of both victims and criminals.

He was in London listening to Archbishop Desmond Tutu, the keynote speaker for this amazing project which had people from all different backgrounds involved. The Archbishop talked about the Truth and Reconciliation hearings in South Africa which took place after Apartheid had broken down. They brought together the police and the army along with the families of the victims of major crimes. In these hearings they talked openly about murder, torture and other horrific things that had taken place during Apartheid. It's an amazing talk from Tutu, the speech itself is a masterclass in storytelling, with great pauses and a slow delivery that draws people in[10]. Richard was in the audience that day when Tutu delivered his speech. He was stuck in the middle of a row in the middle of the audience and as the Archbishop finished the organisers said "The Archbishop needs to leave now, so please remain seated".

10. Yes, you've guessed it, it is on my resources page too – http://bit.ly/GetGoodPresExtras

Everyone stayed seated apart from Richard who thought to himself "I need to talk to him", he stood up in the middle of the row and fought his way past people (in that awkward way you do in the cinema when you trying to get out). He rushed out of the building to find the Archbishop walking down the steps towards his car.

"Excuse me!" Richard said.

Tutu stopped half way down the steps, turned around and said

"Yes?"

Richard replied:

"You don't know what you've just done – you've just helped me forgive the man that murdered my mum when I was a young boy."

He looked at Richard, paused for a few seconds and threw his arms around him. They hugged like a good father hugs his son and went their separate ways.

That was a life changing day for Richard, for his family and for many others.

That's the power of story, that's how a talk can change someone's life.

That's why you should tell your stories too.

Call to Action

What is your call to action?

I think that unless your talk is purely academic, most presentations need to have a call to action at the end.

Always be thinking what I am going to ask people to do?

What will change their behaviour to change the way they think?

What is my call to action?

It might be to buy your product, it might be to invest in your charity, it might be to simply sign up to a website or a course that you have planned. What is your call to action?

Don't let your audience just stew, but at some point, maybe towards the end but not right at the end, give a call to action.

Something like:

"You have heard what I said today…"

"What I would love you to do is…"

"Stop and think now and write one thing down that you are going to change…"

"How has what you have heard today going to affect you?"

However that statement is phrased, make sure you include a call to action. When people do something differently because of what you have spoken about, they will remember you and that's how new business is created. That's how people's lives are changed.

One of the ways to have a call to action is to use a technique that Nancy Duarte uses in her book 'Resonate'. She talks about 'what is' and 'what could be', and has developed this great technique just with a simple diagram like the one below.

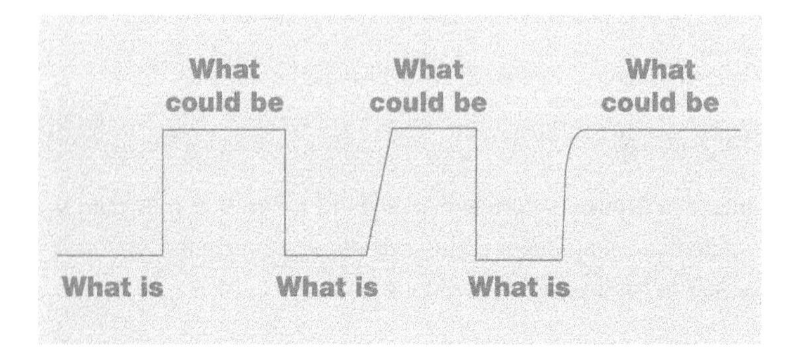

She initially used the 'I Have a Dream' speech by Martin Luther King, but she says it can be used in many different ways. It's a really effective way of thinking about the structure of your talk and your call to action.

Firstly you talk about how things are now, that's at the bottom of the curve, then at the top of the curve is how things could be. This is where we are right now but this is what could happen.

For example, if you work for a charity that deals with homelessness you could say this is the situation at the moment, there are xxxx number of people sleeping rough on the streets, look at what we could do with this new project that we launched last year. We have got xxx number of people from sleeping rough into accommodation, but that only lasted 6 months and now sadly it's gone back to where it was. But, if you could help with funding we could make that difference together. What impact could we have together?

It's the same with a business proposition – what is the problem or the pain that you are solving?

If you watch Dragons' Den (or any other business program where people have to pitch) you will see the biggest criticism is not finances that don't work, the biggest criticism from investors is that people invent something that isn't actually needed. It's very nice to invent a toaster that plays classical music when you make your toast, but actually I am quite happy with my standard toaster so why would I back and fund that?!

We have to find a real problem to solve, showing both the problem and the solution.

Use the diagram to make a difference in your preparation and delivery and the call to action will naturally come out in your presentation. Look for the peaks and the troughs and your call to action will become a much more natural thread running through the talk that you develop.

Less is More

When you walk into an Apple Store one of the things that strikes you is that there is no till – no place to queue up and buy something. The first time I went in it kind of freaked me out a bit. "How do you buy stuff in this store?" There is only shelving for accessories, otherwise it looked plain, simple and uncluttered. Plain desks with computers, iPads and iPhones on display and nothing else – even the leads are all hidden away. Now, because the till didn't exist, it took me a while to understand the process. There were staff floating around who asked "Can get that for you?" They got their little iPad out and I bought my phone lead there and then. They even emailed me the receipt so there was no physical receipt anymore.

Less is more.

The same goes for talks. As I mentioned before, people usually need to lose a third or more of their content, even more if it's particularly dense material. Lose content, lose the stuff that's extraneous to what you REALLY need to present. Remember no one has ever complained if a speech finished earlier than expected![11]

Overrunning speeches are the norm at conferences. No matter who you are you're not going to be anyone's friend if you make them late for coffee or even worse lunch. They all have to get away, people start getting itchy around coffee time, lunch time and going home time at conferences, so keep things short, go up to your time or even better finish a little earlier, take some questions, and finish.

11. Unless you are on live TV I guess, but even then they will probably fill it in!

I am aware that to prevent the risk of overrunning, I have to be ready to ditch parts of my talks in the moment. This is always tricky but can be done with practice. Because I tend to over plan I will always have more content than I was expecting, so I have to make quick decisions while watching the clock and thinking "I am going to ditch that", "I won't use that story" or "I will speed that bit up" and "I will skip over that". You can do this too, particularly if you know your content well, so you never need to overrun and can keep it briefer than you think it needs to be.

Taking Questions

Never take questions at the end, instead take them near to the end and have a few lines planned to finish well, because if you are not careful your whole talk can be hijacked by someone who is a bit grumpy, disagrees with you or is just keen to ask tough questions to show off! It happens.

When you take questions it can really show your expertise, almost more than your talk does, but keep them fairly brief. And if you don't know the answers you can just tell them that and get back to them later.

After a Q&A I always finish with a particular story that wraps up everything and often use a prop as well. It's a funny story with a nice ending, it's like coming in to land.

Get Good

We all need to practice our delivery in order to get good.

That is absolutely true, but not every kind of practice is actually beneficial.

Let's get rid of the phrase "Practice makes Perfect."

Our goal is never perfection.

If you want to make yourself more anxious, then you set your goal as perfection. If you want to be a better speaker let me suggest another way.

Anyone who tries to speak perfectly is destined to fail, it will come across as stilted and forced and it won't engage an audience.

My opinion is simple, perfection is never the goal but getting good is.

You can get good in several different ways but the best way is to do it. Get on your feet and do it.

I get emails every now and again from people who say "how do I become a professional speaker Lee?" or "how do I speak better?". To be honest I just say get out there and do it!

Just speak everywhere you can. I have been speaking since I was 18 years old, in many varied and different contexts. You get good by being on your feet and doing the same talk several times so that you get to feel the nuances of the talk, where the humour fits and which bits really work well. You learn the funny chunks, the more moving chunks and the chunks where you need to pause. This all comes from getting good and that means simply getting on your feet more; speak in front of your family, speak in the local Women's Institute, speak at churches, discussion groups, youth groups, community groups and anybody that will have you. Business breakfasts and Rotary groups are often looking for speakers, just get out there and get in there and get good. Let me explain how that works.

You may have heard about the British Cycling team and the work that Sir Dave Brailsford did there from 2002 onwards. He made the expression 'marginal gains' commonplace. It is basically an applied and anglicised version of the Japanese Kaizen process for performance and process improvement.

Whatever you may think about this process, it is very helpful when learning about presenting.

We can't be a novice speaker one minute and suddenly jump straight to becoming a fantastic speaker the next, that is never going to happen.

We all need to have experience on our feet, we learn to get good bit by bit. In other words you can't jump from novice to expert, you go from novice to slightly less novice, to OK. Then you start to build up the experience of time on stage, different venue types and sizes, you begin to say I have done a community group now, I have done one with café style seating, I have done one with theatre style seating. I have spoken a school hall, I have done a business breakfast, and eventually you get good by adding up all of these little bits of experience, which are marginal gains. As a result of all that experience we make adjustments along the way which helps us become better.

Please, please, please don't practice in front of a mirror! It probably won't help. I think it's one of the two bits of bad advice that people give all the time about presenting. The first is "practice in front of a mirror" and the second one bizarrely is, "if you're nervous imagine your audience are all on the toilet!". I've never quite understood that advice, but I've heard it.

Don't practice in front of a mirror, but practice parts of your talk in your car or when you are walking around. Lots of people do that. Frankie Howard, a comedian from the 80's lived in the countryside and he would do his latest monologues to the cows in the fields nearby! He would walk in the fields, speak to the cows and get feedback from them, there is a documentary of him doing it. Understand that speakers do practice but they tend to practice more on their feet, and try stuff out in front of others.

We are all too close to our material and we need to use that 'try-out stage' of developing our material on our feet. It is not always possible, but if you have the chance, do it. Comedians often do warm up gigs and most people seldom see these but I have seen a couple of big name comedians when they have been getting ready for big arena gigs in small venues where they try out their new material. I once saw Michael Macintyre, who is one of the biggest comedians in the world right now, doing a warm up gig. They introduced him "Please welcome Michael Macintyre" we gave him a round of applause and this guy in a slightly messy and creased suit shuffled onto the stage with his glasses on looking a bit puzzled. He said hello and then read some stuff from a handful of notes he had, he went through pages of little lines and gags and everywhere he got a laugh he picked up the piece of paper and wrote it down. But when you see Michael Macintyre on TV or live he is polished, he is funny, he uses little looks to the crowd for extra laughs, he is super slick, but in this try out gig he was literally just saying the words and seeing what landed – that's how he gets good. It was the same with John Bishop, I have seen him do a warm up gig too. He did some material which was OK and then he started picking on someone in the audience because they heckled him. Comedian's love that and he kind of went for this person and at the same time found a bit of comedy gold during the interaction with a slightly drunk member of the audience. I guess that's what he learnt from the night and he wrote it down. He was improvising, taking risks and enjoying himself, because he knows that his best stuff comes by accident while he is on his feet, not in a sealed room with a laptop.

Everyone is different of course, but there is no replacing time on stage.

One of my favourite comedians is Ken Dodd. Ken is at least 127[12] years old. I met him one night after waiting backstage until about 1.30am with 3 others standing in the freezing cold outside of Leeds Theatre Royal. He eventually came out and shook my hand and I got a chance to chat to him for a while, I asked him "What do you say to people who say they want to be comedians", he said " I tell them to go out there and 'comede'!".

Everyone has to get good somehow, it's just that we don't see people doing it so we presume people have just launched themselves into

12. This may not be strictly true!

the big wide world and become a great speaker. That's not how it works. Find a way to practice that works for you – I even had a friend of mine who came to test a talk at my house once. We set out some chairs in my living room and we invited my elderly neighbours round and 4 of us sat on chairs, we put soft toys on the other chairs and he did his whole talk in front of us! It was bizarre, but it worked for him. So, do whatever works for you.

Don't just practice it in your head, get out there and see the whites of their eyes, because that's when you know what really works.

Enjoy the journey of getting good.

Hands and gestures

Our hands are important to presenting but people get all tied up and in their anxiety don't know what to do with them. I've seen people do odd things like interlace their fingers very specifically or put them high above their hips on their back, or in the worst-case scenario they fold their arms which makes them look negative, nervous and very closed off.

So what do you do with your hands?

The simple answer is to let them fall by your sides, if you are not sure what to do just let them fall naturally by your side and as you speak raise them like you do in normal conversation. You will find that after a bit of thought you start to use gestures normally, don't do anything odd, out of place or repeated movements. Be careful of anxiety and nerves which makes your head make your hands do odd things like clenching your fists, pulling on your left ear lobe or scratching the right hand side of your nose for no apparent reason as I saw one speaker do. If you feel very aware of your hands and start to over think where they should be, just let them fall.

For men, it's a little easier as we tend to wear a fairly standard shirt and trousers combo so its ok to put one hand in your pocket occasionally, I think that can make us look fairly relaxed as long it doesn't go too deep into the pocket which looks very odd! For women it can be more complicated, they might have a dress on or a skirt with no pockets, then what you do with your hands is tricky. It is much easier when you are wearing trousers that are fairly loose where you have got the option of just placing your hand or a thumb into your pocket, for everyone else, seriously, just let them fall.

You might have a clicker in your hand for your slides that will use one hand. Be careful and don't carry papers in your hand, instead put them on a table nearby. If you don't and you are nervous you will end up rattling the paper and that's really off putting. If in doubt just learn to use your hands naturally. The bigger the audience the larger the gestures will need to be, without them being forced.

If you are speaking in a boardroom sized room with say, 8 people, keep your gestures to a minimum, use lots of smiling and eye contact but keep the gestures minimalist otherwise they will feel too big to the audience and it will become overpowering.

If in doubt let your hands fall.

Mr Grumpy should be left at home

I loved the Mister Men cartoons, I remember them well and collected them. One of my favourites was Mr Grumpy. We all have our grumpy days, I have been called grumpy myself, I am sure you have too. But leave Mr Grumpy at home when you are speaking. It's really good to smile and make your facial expression as friendly as possible when speaking – unless of course you are delivering extremely bad news. But on the whole you want to have a nice smile and open gestures. My natural resting face is probably fairly grumpy to be honest, so I have to make an effort to make sure that I look fairly smiley and engage when I am speaking because if I'm not careful I think I can look a little fierce, even though I'm not. Check your resting face in the mirror, just don't practice there as you know!

Get some Video of yourself speaking

Oh yes – video, everybody hates it but it's the most effective tool you will ever use – watching yourself speaking on video is the best way of giving yourself the feedback that you need! Yes, I know we don't like the sound of our own voice, yes we don't like listening and watching ourselves speak but that's how you get the best feedback.

To be honest if anyone loves watching video of themselves they'd have to be pretty narcissistic!

Just get over it, I had to. I once had to spend two days watching my own videos to make my speakers show reel – what a two days that was! It has to be done, just like tax returns!

Audio is good but video is even better, I use it a lot to show delegates what they really look like because as they see it the light suddenly goes on in their heads and they can make adjustments. Then, if you look like me and have got a semi-stern resting face you will know what to do about it.

So the smile, or at least not being Mr or Miss Grumpy, will help you engage an audience because there is so much more to the words than just what we say. A smile really is in your eyes as well as your mouth, it's your eyes that make a difference. So work on it, and get into a good place before taking to the stage, more on that later. Don't be afraid to change your facial expression too depending on which part of the talk you are doing and how you want to engage the audience, experiment with it, just be authentic, be natural, it'll work.

Body language – We cannot not communicate!

One of my favourite photographs is above – "Three Strangers" By Air Adam Photography (used here with kind permission) is shot outside of Leeds Market in West Yorkshire, U.K.

I love this photograph.

Officially these guys are saying nothing but they are communicating.

What do you think they are saying?

How are they feeling?

What kind of day are they having?

Our bodies leak communication all the time. I haven't studied body language academically, but there are things that we can see easily. Obviously folding our arms when speaking is a no no, unless we are becoming a character for a few seconds, but also there are other defensive looking poses too that can create a barrier between us and our audience. People can do all sorts of things to make themselves look uncomfortable on stage. I see people clasp their hands together behind their back, they think it makes them look relaxed but when you show them a video of it, it makes them look really tense. It's the equivalent of folding your arms but with your hands behind your back. It makes your shoulders, neck and chest look tense and can be really uncomfortable. To keep people engaged and receptive we have to have open body postures, open palms are key. The open palm is an international symbol of 'I am not armed' 'I am not dangerous', 'I am going to help you' 'I am on your side'.

It is impossible not to communicate, just like these guys.

"You can either do a show
at the audience
or with the audience"

Ken Dodd

Be 125%

This % could really wind you up particularly if you love numbers and spreadsheets, because of course it doesn't really exist. I hate it when footballers say "I gave it 110%" we can only give 100% – that's how things work.

This % though is about the way that we are when we are delivering.

I believe we should be 100% ourselves but also we need to be 25% bigger for the stage.

Don't be afraid to be that little bit bigger, the most boring speakers in the world are those who become smaller when they speak, those who hide behind their laptop, lectern or stilted script. We should always be bigger on stage than we are in real life.

This became very apparent a long time ago when my wife and I were doing a youth weekend away. We had been invited by a youth worker to take the young people away, doing activities during the day and speaking and hosting in the evening. We kept them entertained all weekend, playing video clips, messy games and little talks – that kind of thing. We ate with the young people at mealtimes too to build relationships. We were sitting round the table with 8 or 9 teenagers and one of them said to my wife Clare "Lee is so funny, you must just laugh all the time at home" Clare burst out laughing! "Yeah of course he is like that all the time in our house!".

They didn't realise that you have to be bigger for the stage, you have to be a bit more interesting, a bit bigger, bolder and funnier. Clare put them right of course! When I am up front I am still me but no matter what kind of talk I do there is an element of performance. I am being myself but a little bit bigger – my stories are a bit bigger, I don't lie but add a little embellishment and remove details or change unimportant facts because it makes it more interesting. I don't make anything up or pretend I was somebody else but when I am telling the story it is important that it is bigger than it actually was at the time. Movies, as they say, are just like life but with all the boring bits taken out. It's the same for speaking. Being bigger and bolder is a part of being a great speaker. Being a little bit extra on stage makes a big difference.

Doing a talk is putting on a show. If you recognise that it's a show and that you are performing in some way it will help you to step up your game. I am not saying that if you are delivering a financial report it needs to be an all-singing, all dancing show, but if you have an attitude of 'how can I entertain and engage people?' it changes everything. It changes your preparation and your delivery.

A few years ago on Britain's Got Talent there was a drummer. He put on a backing track of a famous song and basically drummed along to the song, that was all he did. I was expecting something more. There wasn't anything more. I think he even got into the semi-finals and all he did was play along but he did it in such a way that people loved it, he was smiling, laughing and throwing his sticks in the air, he was spinning around and doing great drum fills, he was putting on a show, basically delivering something fairly boring, but in an interesting way. His attitude of 'I am here to put on a show' changed everything and moved him into the final stages of a competition which he probably should never have got through to.

Don't just do a talk – put on a show. Be yourself but add 25%.

> "Never deliver a talk that you wouldn't want to sit through yourself."
> **Nancy Duarte**

Engage – don't just deliver

That's really what I mean when I say to put on a show. We are there to create engagement we are not just a delivery mechanism. We are not delivering blank, meaningless, emotionless, pieces of information. We are delivering things which people need to hear and hopefully act upon too.

One of the main problems with speakers is that they simply forget about their audience. We can become so obsessed with ourselves, our script, the expectations on us, what we are wearing, our hair, our watch, our shoes, what our hair looks like, we can become obsessed and quite unintentionally narcissistic when we are presenting. That doesn't help our anxiety to be honest but mainly it doesn't help our audience. Our focus should always be "what do they need from me today?" not just "what have I got to deliver to them?"

Even if you are delivering mandated and legally binding content like at a work induction day, we still must focus on *them* and not on *us*.There is always tension around what do they *need* from me and what do I need to *deliver*, but as soon as we drift into 'I have to do this and I know it is boring' for more than a few minutes then we have lost the audience.

If there is a dull bit, put something in that section to make it less dull, insert a story, do a quiz, get some interaction from them and find a way that they can be engaged in what you are saying.

Our key focus here is to understand that we are using the time of every audience member, something they will never get back – 200 people in the room for one hour is 200 hours of time that the world will never get back. So, use that time wisely, it's precious – think what do they need from me?

Bad musicians can teach speakers a lot

I have spent most of my life loving music and being a musician, playing in bands and being a DJ /producer over many years. I love music of lots of different genres and as I get older I have developed more of an eclectic taste from my old school hip hop roots right through to all sorts of music now, both old and modern. I love playing it in the car when I'm on my own and have just had my old record deck re-installed in my home. I like discovering new music and often go back to the stuff I've always loved too. I have lots of playlists on my iPhone of my favourite songs. Once you make music you understand how it is created, particularly if you do production and performing as I did. You learn the little skills that make music sound great and realise when you hear an amateur musician or bad band how different they sound to the real pros. I've even had friends give me music they've created and I hoped they didn't ask me for feedback (!). Everyone has to start somewhere but new musicians often make bad music, it is all part of the process of getting good.

One of the reasons that an amateur band sounds different from a professional band is because they play every note on the page. I used to play in a band with a guy who was learning to play an instrument and would play every single note without feeling, in a very regimented style. It had no soul, it was literally the notes on the page and added nothing to the overall feel.

When I have watched some of my professional friends play, I realise how little they actually play but how much they add to the overall sound.

Doing a talk is not about playing every note, everything you know or have researched. Sure there is a science to presenting but there is also an art. Part of that art is to allow the space to live, allow yourself to play with the material and with the audience a little bit, pausing, changes of direction, little looks, little asides, little improvisations. We don't have to and should not 'play every 'note on the page'.

I take lots of notes before I present and do lots of research I often have some notes with me on the stage, particularly for longer presentations, but I rarely use them while in the flow. If I was to read out everything on the page it would be the dullest thing in the world – the notes help to keep me on track sometimes, especially if I am doing something new. I've have had to pick and choose what I need to include, even deciding I don't need to do that bit now/anymore. That's why audiences hate death by PowerPoint because very big slide decks are linear and seem unmovable, there is a feeling that the speaker has to get through all the slides so they inflict them on the audience and don't realise that actually they could just pause and skip 2 or 3 slides. In fact, if you know the slide number you want, in PowerPoint, or other software, you can jump to a desired slide while your slides are playing, type in the number for a prepared black slide or press the 'B' button to go to a blank black slide. Then without any fuss you have the freedom and ability to change course. You don't have to play every note, you can blank the slide, you can allow a pause, maybe do some reflection and allow the audience to interact with some questions.

Great music

If you want to see this in real music terms then have a listen to "Don't Stop till you Get Enough" by Michael Jackson or "Superstition" by Stevie Wonder, (they are on the resources webpage for you here – http://bit.ly/GetGoodPresExtras). Listen to the fantastic pauses in these songs, the pauses make the space and the gaps make the song. They don't have to try too hard or play every note.

"If passion drives you,
let reason hold the reins."
Benjamin Franklin

Positivity, Passion and Enthusiasm

There are many ways to sell your message to an audience, to help you to engage with them and to help them to engage with you.

Being positive is one of the main ways to keep engagement.

Even when delivering bad news there are still ways to be positive, as long as we read the room well and are not inappropriate.

There are always ways to see the light at the end of tunnel and the right way forward. No one wants doom and gloom, they want us to find solutions. I have been to training events with a 'state of the nation' type session – they have discussed where they are as a company, what is the world looking like, what are the big issues. Those kind of sessions can easily become depressing and it's important to present those sessions positively. I even got a couple of laughs and sweet smiles while doing my Dad's and Uncle's eulogies at their funerals. It wasn't as inappropriate as it sounds, it was actually quite helpful for the audience, or so they told me. This isn't denying the grieving process, far from it, but it can be helpful to go into every talk with an appropriate sense of positivity. People need hope and as speakers we are privileged to be able to give them that occasionally.

Enthusiasm sells too

Be enthusiastic – people can connect with that. If they know that you enjoy what you are talking about that comes across quickly. They shouldn't need to listen to you for an hour to get that. I have listened to talks in all sorts of different contexts. In my work in the NHS I have listened to people talking about haematology (working with blood). It's not something that I want to work with or that I know anything about, (particularly with my squeamish nature), but their passion and enthusiasm came across and I was left thinking 'I get it' 'I get what they do', 'they love it'. It may not be my field of work or specialty, but for them it is what they do and they know it makes a difference. I was swept away with their enthusiasm about their subject.

Passion

There is a danger with passion. It is a great thing and it is important, but passion should never be so big that it removes rationality and good research. We could become passionate about something that just isn't true – so be very careful..

Let your passion come out, make sure you have done your research and make sure you know what you are talking about – that's when passion can sell well. It's key to getting across a message.

Like anything, it can be overdone, it can look fake and you can lose credibility if passion trumps your experience and research. Don't ever apologise for being passionate. I have heard people say "I make no apology for my passion today" which in effect is saying "I am making an apology for my passion today" or that's how it appears. If you are saying "I am making no apology" then you actually are making an apology – just let people see your passion and they will respond to that, not everyone will love it and love you, but who cares, it is far better to be passionate than boring, monotone and deliberately dull.

Props

Using props in presentations can be really helpful and a good alternative to dull slides. Slides have killed the use of props. I reckon it is time to bring them back.

What can you use that would help?

What could you show to the audience during your delivery that would help you to get a key point across?

I have three big prop boxes in my office. The best places to buy them are discount shops, car boot sales, online auction sites, kid's toy shops and charity shops.

If there are 3 main points in your talk, could you attach a prop to one of those points to make it more memorable? E.g. if you are talking about the brain get a fake sponge brain. I know of people who have given a talk about the power of words over people's lives and they used an actual cows tongue from the butchers, they kept it in the fridge and brought it in a box and showed the tongue of the cow! That is something pretty memorable!

Learning to use props is about a change in mind-set too, so that when you are out and about, not only are you looking for things to write down for your Tickle files, but you are also thinking "oh I can use that prop". If you do one talk a lot you probably need to have a box for that talk, so you will take with you a projector, laptop, some notes, pens and your props too. I have a case that has all of my technical stuff in it but it is also big enough to fit my main props in too. If it's a shared presentation that maybe you and your colleagues do then make that prop box a shared resource, have a checklist on the box and take it with you every time you do that talk. It makes life easier.

The other thing about props is to learn how to use them, it's no good just lifting it up quickly and putting it back down again – you have to allow the audience to see it. Hold it up with an outstretched arm in front of you and let the audience see it clearly, don't just kind of fumble it out of your bag and say "there you go" and drop it back in your box. Allow the 'show' to be a pause in your delivery, allow it to be something they take in.

Presenting them well is half the battle with props. I have different versions of my main props too, I have big versions and smaller versions because when I am travelling on a train I may not have the space to take big props with me, whereas a smaller one works better. Be creative and let your brain go wild thinking of the props that you could use.

Use props to get away from too many slides and using just your voice. Having worked with many clients in different workplaces, I am pretty sure that most talks we do could have at least one prop to make it more memorable.

I challenge you to use one in your next presentation.

Another example: When people ask me to talk about slides, I will sometimes take a crutch with me, it's from an old set of crutches that my Mum used to use. As I talk about slides being a crutch for people, instead of just saying they are a crutch, I actually show a crutch, hold it up in front of me so everyone can see it and as I speak more about it I start to lean on it.

A prop can reinforce the words you say. A prop makes you more memorable.

If you are a great speaker you want to be memorable, to be trusted, to be re-booked, and to be noticed. That is natural and goes against the grain of the industry standard of the corporate camouflage of Death-by-PowerPoint.

Can they apply what you are saying?

There should be some kind of way of people applying the advice or expertise you are giving them.

As you are speaking to people, think 'how can they apply this now, tomorrow or when they get back to work?' That process of asking what the application is rather than just making them think, could make the difference between delivering a practical or an abstract talk. An abstract talk I define as one that was nice to hear but won't make much of a difference to me. It just hangs there briefly and gets lost in the noise of my life. The kind of talk where we shrug at the end of it and then move on quickly to the coffee break.

Think:

What do they need to do to apply what I've said?

How long will it take?

What equipment do they need?

How can they implement this today?

For example if you are speaking on time management you can say to them:

"It's as simple as this, tomorrow morning before you do anything else – get a piece of paper and write down the three things you need to do before anything else".

"Write that every day and watch how your productivity grows".

"A free PDF of a sheet for you to use is here [give them a practical thing to take away and download]......."

That is simple advice around productivity but you can see how it becomes very practical:

"get a pen"

"a piece of paper"

"before you do anything else..."

This is practical stuff, not just 17 abstract points on productivity.

How can you make people apply what you say to them?

Get Help. Get Feedback

But choose carefully.

If you work as part of a team, whenever you are preparing or delivering your material, practice it in front of real people and give them an idea of what you would say, or maybe just run an idea by them "I am thinking about speaking about this" "I saw this the other day what do you think?" Deliberately ask for feedback. As they say, feedback is the breakfast of champions, it is good to have.

What can you do to get feedback and help?

Who should you ask?

Who would be encouraging but also honest?

Do you need a Presentation Coach?

If you work on your own as I often do, it is more tricky, that's one reason I joined the PSA (The Professional Speaking Association) and it's also the reason why I seek out other speakers too. I will ring them up, or have a video call and say "look I have got this idea – what do you think?" "Do you think that will work?" "If I say it like this instead, is it better?" I will do little sections of my new talks too because being alone in our own head is not good for us when getting ready to deliver, we have got to get help from other people.

Is a funny thing though!

How do you process it? How does it make you feel?

As a speaker I get feedback all the time, both written and verbal. I once met a fellow speaker at his office, he had big piles of A4 feedback sheets from recent events all over the floor of his office, there was half a tree's worth on his office floor! It's just part of my world.

Recently after doing two speaking events for speaker bookers where I was there to receive feedback (and bookings), the tables were turned when on the Saturday of that week I became the judge for a speaking competition and had to give feedback to other speakers! It's a tricky thing to give feedback, especially to new speakers who need encouragement and constructive feedback to help them improve.

A healthy balance is key.

Feedback is a lot easier to give it out, than to receive for most people.

Some people I've met run away from feedback as they've been hurt in the past by a boss who was blunt, manipulative or just a poor people person. But even if we have had bad experiences, it is part of life now and we need to find a way to process it.

Here are my 5 tips on dealing with feedback of any sort.

My feedback on feedback!

1. Learn to sieve it!

I've learned to listen to all feedback but to sieve it very thoroughly in my head, sometimes even while it's being given to me! Feedback comes with baggage, so ask – who's giving me this? Why are they giving me this? What are their motives? Keep sieving and you can disregard and take on board some, but not all. I did a training day for a company once and the feedback was strangely mixed. I was shocked to be honest as I thought it had gone well and the verbal feedback on the day was great. But the written feedback we got a few days later was decidedly mixed. So I decided to process it properly. I wrote down the feedback that I was concerned about, reflected on it, spoke to my colleagues and eventually I realised that this just didn't seem right. So, I called the CEO who'd booked me and had a chat. I told her that I was concerned about the mixed feedback as this usually didn't happen. We talked for ten minutes and the penny dropped. She told me that the feedback sheets were not done until a few days after and in an open office (maybe even around the water cooler). She also said that some of the delegates were recently retired from an industry that is known for very harsh feedback. I got the impression that some of them didn't like any training at all and didn't want to be there anyway, especially as they were used to working independently and only saw each other a few times a year. They were also used to giving training, not receiving it. The CEO then assured me that she was very happy with the day and would use me again in the future. Phew! If I hadn't processed that properly and hadn't made that call, then I'd never have known the truth behind the unusual feedback. Keep sieving!

2. Not everyone's opinion really matters

This seems harsh I know, but it's true. I have seen new speakers give other new speakers long and detailed feedback as if they are experts. Their feedback as a human being is perfectly valid of course, but unless they are experienced in that field, it's just not as valuable as someone who's been speaking successfully for years. I personally listen to feedback from speakers who I respect, and I've changed bits of my talks as a result, but that group is a select few. Everyone's opinion is valid but it doesn't always carry the same weight and impact.

3. Don't take it personally

This is a challenging one, but if you want to keep on going it's essential. If you get feedback on a work issue, it's work, not usually a personal attack. Just because someone says that your talk isn't as good as it should be doesn't mean that you are a bad person. It means that you may need some more training or you need more experience. Play to your strengths more. It's business not personal. Getting that into perspective really helps. Life is challenging enough without battering our self-esteem with stuff that isn't relevant.

4. Ask yourself, is this true?

Some feedback is right and proper. Some feedback we should take on board, it's what makes us better at our job or helps us become a better person. Self-awareness is the key to personal and professional growth and part of that is being able to say, "Yeah they were right, I need to change that". When I teach presentation skills I always make a point to say at the beginning of the session "I'm a pretty nice person, I'll make this fun today, you will get chocolate (!), but you need to know that I will give you direct feedback too, because we all need it to get better. Please don't be offended, it's just feedback...". Once they know that, they seem to relax more and at the end of the session they always come out as better speakers, some even grow and become more confident generally – that's why I love teaching presentation skills. A while ago I was coaching a group and during the final speeches one delegate was using a scrappy, folded A4 sheet for notes, but it was becoming a distraction. So I stopped the talk mid-flow and took the piece of paper from her. She carried on and nailed the talk, of course she didn't need the piece of paper, she didn't need notes, but without that feedback that leader would probably continue to use a sheet of A4 notes for the rest of her professional life! She didn't need them, she was great. She took it onboard and simply got better. It was a privilege to see someone take feedback without offence. Sometimes we have to do that, it's part of our job.

And lastly:

5. It's not the full picture

The other thing about feedback is that often I can be speaking to a room of 200+ people and only chat to three people afterwards, so you never know what people take away. I received the emails below previously from events where I got little or no feedback at the time. These are keepers for me:

After a business event, where, if I'm honest, the talk seemed like "hard work" – I got this:

"Hi Lee, Just had to drop you a line to say a big thank you again. I've had a couple of emails through saying how much they enjoyed your talk. I don't normally get this! You obviously did something right!"

So it turned out that the audience just weren't very responsive – it was personality types, that is all. They loved it, but as an extrovert I didn't see it like that!

And after a talk in a challenging school, I got this email:

"Dear Lee, My name is ________. You spoke at my school ________. I don't think you remember me but we talked after your talk and all I would like to say to you is thank you. You really changed the way I thought of my exams, well I have finished my exams and school altogether. I have started listening to your book 'How to enjoy and succeed at school and college'. And I am really loving the book. I have enrolled in ________college..."

He then went on to ask me a question about something I'd said in my talk. It made my day.

Feedback: Collect it, use it, process it wisely, read it when you need to, but don't live your life for it, or under it!

If you are interested in more about the PSA you can find the details at www.thepsa.co.uk/join, seek out others to get help and you will get better every time.

Speaking is a solo sport on stage but you need a team to get you there.

Some quick fire delivery tips

- **One minute rule** – Grab people's attention in the first minute or you have lost them. Say something (appropriate!) to 'get them back in the room'. Don't forget you can introduce yourself a few minutes in – it doesn't have to be right at the beginning.
- **Use your accent** – Let your regional accent shine through, it could be your greatest asset. Ham it up if you have to, find the key words that make you stand out from the crowd.
- **Smarten up** – Dress well and appropriately, or all people may "hear" is the way you are dressed. General rule of thumb is that the speaker should be the best dressed there. Err on the side of caution.
- **Do the lighthouse** – As you speak, naturally look around the room – making sure that you catch everyone's eye for a brief moment, it makes them feel part of your talk, just don't stare for too long as that is weird!
- **Walk well** – Staring at notes or staying behind a lectern is a yawn. Walk around and engage your audience – practice it at the venue beforehand if you can and that will help you enormously.
- **3 Minute warning** – I often ask someone for a 3-minute warning so I have time to wrap up even if I am still in full-flow. Going over time doesn't win you any friends, so be disciplined.
- **End well** – Learn your ending, so you know when to end with a memorable conclusion or call to action.

- **Meat and gravy** – don't forget there has to be 'meat with the gravy' and 'substance with the style' people want more than just froth, otherwise what's the point? Don't be so showy that you forget to deliver great content.

Anxiety

"Non-clinical anxiety is experiencing failure in advance."

Seth Godin

A right state

I'm a speaker, I am not a psychologist or psychiatrist but I have tried to understand anxiety, I have felt it personally, I have seen it in friends and family. I have studied it, chatted to people with it, I've simply tried to understand it more fully.

Seth Godin, I think, hits the nail on the head particularly when it comes to presentation anxiety or speaker nerves.

Being nervous is something that is quite normal, feeling anxiety before standing up in front of 200 people is a normal thing and perfectly natural. It's about 'fight or flight', it's a good thing for our bodies and minds to be at a heightened state of awareness so that we can perform at our best.

But it all depends how we deal with it.

I think lots of things are good things but it depends how we deal with these things.

I am very happy and very thankful for beer! I enjoy a glass of beer though I haven't been drunk for many years to be honest, since I was a teenager – but I do enjoy an occasional glass of beer, it's how we deal with it. I have friends who are alcoholics who can't drink, it's how we deal with it. It is a choice we all make, I choose not to get drunk, my friends who are alcoholics choose to avoid alcohol completely.

I was helping on a Presentation Skills course years ago and Steve McDermott told me the best thing to do with presentation nerves is to help people to get into '**the** right state' not '**a** right state', that has always made me laugh, it's very Yorkshire and I think it's spot on. He even mentioned the idea of Christmas morning as a kid in the 70's/80's, I remember it well. I would be anxious on Christmas morning coming down the stairs ready to open my presents, I guess that was a sense of nervousness but it was a good nervousness. It was akin to "I am ready to rock", "I am ready to inspire", "I am ready to give it my best go" "I am excited" rather than a pre-dentist anxiety feeling of dread. There wasn't a Harry Potter Death Eater following me around sucking the energy out of me, it felt better, easier to handle.

The idea that we get into 'the right state' for ourselves was so helpful to me. To feel a bit more like Christmas morning is my aim now, to have those slight butterflies in my stomach but feeling like I am ready to go can make a difference and really help my performance too.

The fear of failure is a big thing for adults and children alike

Monty Python Comedian John Cleese said that it is the aim of every British person to get to the grave without ever being embarrassed!

What do presentations do? They give us an ideal opportunity to fail and to be embarrassed! So with the combination of Seth Godin's and John Cleese's quotes, it's no wonder that people get nervous speaking.

I definitely think that it's all about a routine (more on that later) and not understanding the difference between our anxiety's perception of the real and the actual real world. Anxiety changes our perception and this is why you get people who become agoraphobic and don't go out of the house because they have had their perception changed about the outside world, what it looks like, and the fears that are there.

I have known enough people with agoraphobia to understand how that would feel – of course the world isn't out to get them but their perception tells them otherwise. So, the best thing to do with anxiety is get the stuff out of your head and into the real world. If we internalise things and become introspective the whole time, we end up always thinking the worst because whenever we look inwardly we can easily think the worst. It is very easy to sit at home, watch the news, read the newspapers and convince ourselves that the world is horrendous and we should never venture into it. This type of thinking is easily done, and that is why we have families, friends and communities to live in – because even the most introverted person needs others' views, perspectives, love, conversations and even just the sunshine and outdoors to live a balanced life.

Don't believe everything you think.

Whenever we are lonely we can easily think the worst and whenever we are with our own thoughts for too long we can go to a pretty dark place quite quickly. That is because there is a difference between 'reality' and 'perceived reality'.

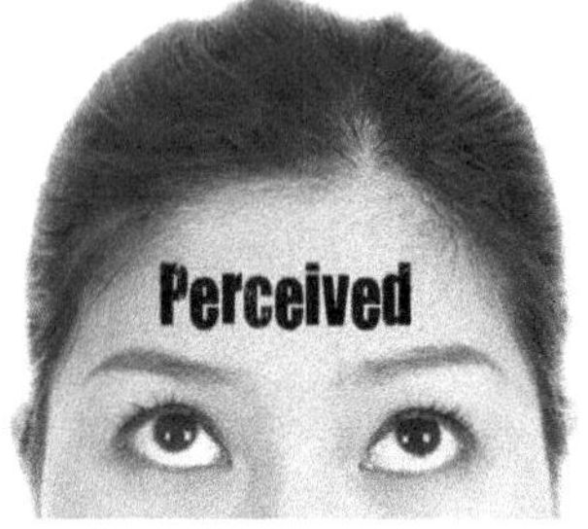

So with that perspective, here are a few things that might help you become less anxious when presenting.

Some ways to 'get your head straight':

1. The audience doesn't want you to fail! No-one who sits in an audience is thinking 'I hope this person is really dull'. What they're actually thinking is 'I hope they are good', 'I hope that they are engaging' and 'I hope I get something from this'. It is **'WIIFM'** (Whats In it For Me) again. People want you to do well – even competitors sometimes. I learned this the hard way. When I was first asked to speak at a PSA conference in front of 100 professional

speakers I was really nervous! Can you imagine speaking for half an hour in front of 100 professionals who do it for a living? I had the attitude of "and little old me has to get up on stage now and just give it a go". What I realised afterwards was that it was one of the best talks that I have ever done! Thankfully I have got it on video too because everybody in the room was a professional speaker and they wanted me to do well! They were willing me to do well, they sit in conferences all the time and didn't want to be bored, they were engaging, they enjoyed my different style, my humour, delivery and content that I had brought. I will never forget that day – that people actually want me (and also you) to do well. The cherry on the cake was that I signed up one of my biggest clients that day. If I hadn't stepped up and fought through my speaker's nerves I would never have learned that lesson and got the paying gigs! It was a red letter day for me, and a few years later (as you may know) – I became the PSA President too. Maybe they just set me up!

2. Have you done your preparation? If you have, then you can rest on that fact. Your good preparation is solid ground to stand on.

3. Have you got any experience in the field you are speaking on? If you have then that is solid ground too. You can rest on that expertise, not arrogantly, but a quiet assurance based on your expertise.

4. One of the most powerful questions that I ask myself is this. "Have I ever done a talk before?" For me the answer is of course "Yes. Hundreds of them." That alone can get me out of my perceived

reality and back into the real world. I say to myself "Of course you have, you've done this kind of thing loads of times Lee", "You have spoken in front of the toughest audiences", "You have done all sorts of presentations from audiences that speak different languages and are from different countries, to primary schools, CEO groups and everything in between". That question, "Have I done this before?", helps me to put things into perspective. "I will be fine, it's not a problem", helps me to get out of my nervous state and get into as Steve says, "the right state". Therefore, reducing my anxiety and helping to feel like I am ready to go, so that my nerves don't destroy what I am doing and what I'm qualified for. Yet another reason to get out there and speak as much as you can – the more experience you have, the more you have to rest upon. The more solid ground you have to build a good routine.

Don't judge the audience with your anxiety!

A real life 'lesson learned that day' story from speaker Michelle Mills-Porter:

I had been booked to speak at a Charities' Christmas bash and they wanted my Human Magnificence story, which is about my experience in the tsunami and it's pretty hard hitting! I was 30 minutes into my hour-long talk and I realised the audience were looking a bit… well…bored! They didn't seem to be engaged and where I was used to gasps, there was silence. Where I was usually got "awwww's" there was nothing. My audience was zombified!

The speech continued, but my inner voice was talking in parallel, "You've lost them, Michelle!...They'll never ask you back." "What were they thinking, booking you?" I found myself losing confidence at a rate of knots and before I knew it I was wrapping up … EARLY!

Never in more than a decade of speaking, had I ever wrapped up early, or late. As I walked back to my seat, my inner voice mocked me…"You haven't given value for money… you finished 10 minutes early! You've never work again!" It got more and more ridiculous.

I leaned into the Director who had booked me, about to apologise for my performance when she said "They LOVED that, Michelle!"

Before I knew it I had a line of people queueing to say how much they enjoyed my talk. They were "Right there with me!" they were "Totally awestruck" and "Captivated!" Then I remembered, they have a certain behaviour profile. They are all caring, nurturing, charitable people whose facial expressions rarely give off what they are really thinking…One of the biggest lessons of my speaking career came with a wave of relief! Lesson learned. Don't panic!

"They look so natural up there"

As I have researched anxiety with performers and speakers it's amazing what you find out. I found that most people, particularly entertainers will talk about this quite a lot in their biographies, e.g. Peter Kay, the Bolton comedian, appears to be one of the most at ease with himself when he is on stage, very down to earth, but in his autobiography, he says how nervous he is and how he is "bricking it" at the side of the stage. It's the same with Ant and Dec the TV presenters, they seem to be easy going presenters who put others at ease, in their element when they are presenting TV shows. Yet, again, in their autobiography they explain that they are very nervous before they go on stage. I found out about the late Sir Bruce Forsyth too, he was a presenter and all-round entertainer for decades. If you have ever seen him on TV you might notice that he did a little skip, just before he starts. It's called the 'Brucie Skip', as he was being interviewed he was asked "why do you do that little skip?" He replied "that skip gets me into the right zone so that I go from being nervous to 'right, I am on it now'". He thinks "I am nervous, I am nervous, I am nervous" and then he does a little skip and, boom, he is in the zone of speaking or presenting. It's funny how we don't notice these things until we look, but even Bruce Forsyth had nerves to deal with and his way of dealing with it was by doing his little skip.

How is the best way to deal with yours?

What would be your equivalent of the 'Brucie skip'?

Expectations

A lot of presentation anxiety not only comes from the fear of failure and embarrassment, but also because people set too high expectations for themselves when they are presenting.

People sometimes want to be the best presenter in the world but the reality for most of us is that we should simply want to enjoy it and make a connection with the audience.

Something as simple as lowering your expectations a little can work wonders.

Yes, I know, I'm a motivational speaker and, yes, I just said to you to lower your expectations!

You are most likely not a professional stand-up comedian or an accomplished and polished speaker. You are most likely someone who is out there to simply present a message well, so for the sake of your mental health, lower your presentation expectations a little.

One of the big expectations that we have, which became very clear in the film "The King's Speech", is that many speakers are overly concerned about being word perfect. There is a lot of anxiety attached to:

"I didn't say that sentence quite right", or "I got mixed up with that particular paragraph/story". I am fully aware that I am not word perfect and neither is this book, but I have learned to live with that, I know that the other skills that I have will get me over that fact. My books and presentations won't be word perfect but that's fine, that's who I am, I get my message across in other ways. I am not fully scripted, I am not an actor who can memorise, I deliver chunks of material that help people and I focus on that.

Don't make it worse for yourself

Watch what you say.

Here's the key:

Don't tell the audience what they don't know!

If you are feeling nervous don't tell them that, if this is your first talk don't tell them that. I have heard all sorts of terrible things said in presentations, "I am not used to doing talks", "I am sorry I am very nervous" "You all look so scary!".

I had heard one person say once "I haven't had time to prepare this morning so I am just going to read from my slides", and the whole audience slumped into their seats at that point. Even worse I heard someone say once "I haven't had time to do any preparation, in fact these aren't even my slides, I have just been given them so I am just going to read through them now."

My jaw dropped.

I wanted to stand up and leave the room along with 200 other people because it was obvious that we were going to be wasting our life away as someone inflicted unprepared Death-by-PowerPoint on us all.

Don't tell people what they don't know, do your preparation, rest on some of your experience and learn to connect more by controlling the way that you think and speak to yourself.

Things will go wrong occasionally – be flexible!

If someone falls off their chair mid-talk, that's happened to me, be flexible.

If the microphone stops working you will get a new battery given to you, or a replacement mic, or you maybe you don't need a mic, it'll be ok, be flexible.

If your slides go down, do the talk without them, you probably know what you are going to say anyway, be flexible.

All sorts of things can go wrong when you speak – that's ok, if you go with the attitude of "I have got the flexibility to keep on going" then that's what you will do. You'll survive!

Once, I was doing a talk in a tough urban school with, to be honest, a pretty bad reputation. They put me in the dining room just after the mayhem of lunch, I was setting up while the students ate their lunch followed by a mad five minutes to turn the room around ready for my talk. As I was speaking the dinner ladies were still scraping plates and wiping tables at the back while chatting.

Twenty minutes into my talk a phone rang loudly and a lad in the audience looked at his phone and silenced it without blinking an eye, I left it and didn't say anything. The teachers gave him 'the look' and I just carried on, then his phone rang loudly again and a teacher started to get up to send him out. But I said "no problem", I went up to the lad and as he got his phone out of his pocket I gently took it out of his hand and I answered it. I said "sorry mate he can't speak to you at the moment, he is listening to a really good speaker that's really going to help him at school". Nobody knew what to say. I gave the lad his phone back and three seconds later it rang again, it was his mate ringing back as he didn't understand who'd answered the last time.

The teachers told me afterwards that from that moment I had really got their attention. It is like they had seen that I had the confidence to deal with unusual events, to be flexible, to go with the flow a bit and after that they really started listening to me. They knew that I wasn't just delivering a script but I was there to help them, it also made the lad think twice about keeping his phone switched on in school too. I look back at that with fondness now and actually hope that someone's phone rings in one of my talks in the future, because I could use that moment, and not panic when it happens.

Be flexible. It's good for you.

There are short term fixes to feeling less nervous (more in the next few pages) but ultimately it is the medium to long term ones that will make the most difference.

What is your routine before you speak?

Do you have one?

Are you aware of it?

Have you ever even thought about it?

The fact is that if you don't think you have a pre-talk routine, you still have a pre-talk routine…

…it's just that you are not conscious of it.

Some things we do, we are not conscious of.

I don't think every morning "How am I going to get up and clean my teeth today?" I just get up and do it, it doesn't take much conscious thought to think about cleaning my teeth but I just do it anyway. It's a routine that I have.

Lots of people that I have helped over the years have discovered that they have a set pre-talk routine that they had no idea about.

I was coaching somebody who was a very nervous speaker a couple of years ago, they had been put up for a national award and they had to give a talk to receive the award in front of lots of high level executives and government officials. As they were told about the award and speech, they were given my details and sent to chat to me. This person's mindset and routine was "I don't like talks" "I don't do talks" "I am not very good at talks" and "I can't do this". This self-talk was very loud in their head and it spilled out as words and feelings as soon as I spoke to them on the phone.

When I met this person face to face and got them to the front of the room they were unable to simply say their name in front of their colleagues and myself. They got themselves into such a bad routine and negative state that they made themselves their own worst enemy. They had a fantastic message to share but their self-talk and unknown, unhealthy routine had really got in the way.

We spent some time on their general preparation and presentation skills and then spent a lot of time talking about anxiety and doing some exercises to help. I am glad to say that they went on to do a fantastic talk and got great feedback, it's one of my proudest moments as a presentation coach. I saw personal and professional development taking place right in front of my eyes that day, they were a different person afterwards. I drove home a happy man that night.

Imagine if someone calls you today and asks if you'll give a talk in a months' time. If your mindset / routine is that you don't particularly enjoy doing talks. Then your instant thought is "I don't want to do it", your brain gets into a negative frame of mind and you start to perpetuate that negative self-talk that I referred to above.

'Self-talk' is the things we say to ourselves, just behind our consciousness, like a looped vocal track playing in the background of our mind.

The power of self-talk can change people's lives and unfortunately bad self-talk about presentations can make us a complete nervous wreck standing on a stage.

Here is how to get a better routine

First of all, realise that you have one, it is not a bad thing, it is just reality, we all have them.

Then secondly try to establish a different pattern, a different mind-set. A different routine.

In order to break a previous routine that creates nerves and anxiety before a talk, little changes make a big difference.

So, if you get asked to do a talk in a months' time, say "Yes, I'll do it", and at that point you have immediately made a positive step and can start to think "Great I will do that talk". Often when I say yes to a presentation, I spend some time very early on doing a bit of preparation. Maybe something jumped into your head straight away? Write it down immediately and then do some notes over the next few days, maybe start to plan like I taught you earlier. I have often spoken to a client on the phone and immediately written down loads of ideas straight after the call, it is like my brain suddenly sparks into life and sets off a chain reaction of creativity, so capture it. Get out the Post-it notes and plan a little bit of the talk in the first few days. That's a positive start and you are not then leaving it all to the last minute. Maybe leave it a week before you continue to think and go back to do a bit more planning, then interrupt your routine by finding out a bit more, ask about the audience, the venue and everything else that you need to know. Then a couple of weeks beforehand, you can start to pull it together and to deliver some of it in front of friends or colleagues.

As the day approaches your new routine really needs to kick in. A couple of days before, make sure you have done your preparation well, you have got everything you need, your props, gadgets, slides, notes or whatever you need for that particular talk. Make sure everything is ready that will help. Find out any more information about the event. How many people are going to be there now? Do they have the correct IT stuff for you? Will there be a table to put some notes on? Think about all the things that you need 'on stage' for your presentation, contact the organiser if you have any other questions too.

I reckon that controlling your environment can reduce anxiety by up to 50%. Often it is the nerves of "I don't know how big the hall is", "Will the audience be sitting café style or theatre style?", "Will I have some water nearby?" All these questions unanswered can increase our anxiety so controlling the environment can be a great part of your new routine.

Now to the night before

If your talk is mid-morning the next day, the night before is often when people say "Oh I don't sleep" because they have got into a bad routine. So make sure you have got everything in place you will need, everything packed and your clothes ready. Make sure you are not stressed out working until midnight or watching the news over and over again, and then have to get up at 6am to travel. Get yourself in a good state. Have a good meal the night before, watch something funny on TV or read a light-hearted book. I often watch funny stuff that will help me to relax in the evening, laughter is great for that. Take a notebook with you on this new routine journey too, take it to bed so if you start thinking about the presentation before you go to sleep or in the night, you can write that stuff down with positive solutions to your thoughts or questions. I always have a notebook by my bed so that if I get ideas that stop me from sleeping I just scribble them down and can pick them up in the morning and deal with them, hopefully this will help you rest and have a good sleep.

On the morning of your talk go through your usual routine, I think you know how to use the bathroom so I won't tell you how to do that! Get yourself ready and turn up at the venue early, not thinking "I'm going to get there early because I am nervous" but early because you want to just double check a couple of things, the microphone, the table and very importantly where are you going to stand? If you get a chance to stand on the stage before anyone turns up, go for it and get the feel and look of what it is like standing on that particular stage. I do that so it's not a new experience for me, it starts to look familiar and feel more like home.

You are establishing a new routine and so be careful what you do beforehand. If your talk is at 10.30 in the morning and there are two talks before you, don't spend all that time on email or dealing with problems at work. Switch off your phone, speak to some friends that you trust or positive people if you need to. Do that to get yourself in the right frame of mind, remind yourself that you have done this before. Some speakers, like athletes, listen to music before they go on stage too, music is very powerful, it changes moods. I also hate to be hemmed in on a row of sets before I speak, so I tend to hang about at the back on a chair or even stand up so I can nip out easily to stretch my legs and walk around the venue.

My little black book

I have a little book of notes where I keep copies of testimonials from clients and nice things that people have said about me, and sometimes if I need to, I will read it to get me into 'the right state'. It is a private book, no one else sees it apart from me. It is full of testimonials, little notes from my kids and wife and quotes and things that make it easy for me to get into the right frame of mind and remind myself once again, I have done this hundreds of times so "just get on with it Lee"!

Do what you need to, to help you to get yourself out there ready to go.

Just before you go on stage have in mind your first line, what's the first thing you are going to say, the first few lines in your head are usually all you need, because once you have that sorted, you will find that everything else will flow.

There you go we have established a new routine! You might need to write down your new routine. You might need to check yourself when someone asks you to do a talk in case you start to get negative about it and start to run negative self-talk. You might decide not to speak to certain people who will bring you down too. You need encouragers not people who'll say "Yeah I hate talks too – this awful thing happened to me..." to get you into a good routine. Find out what works and then establish that well so that it becomes a natural pattern for you to make into a routine.

The only thing we can control to a certain extent is our own brains, and that's what you can do with presentation anxiety – control your own reactions, your own internal thoughts and perceived reality to get yourself into the right frame of mind to deliver well.

And of course the great thing about routines is that once you have established a good one it will become second nature to you over time, reason 4657 why you should do as many talks as you can. Speak more to establish good routines.

Here are a few other little tips that might help you be less nervous:

Don't forget to breathe!

Breathing is really important (obvious fact of the day, Lee!), when we are anxious if we are not careful we can start to breathe quicker and more shallowly and we breath just from the top of our lungs. This creates more anxiety and becomes a circle of "I'm feeling nervous so I breathe shallowly and because I'm breathing shallowly I feel more nervous". To break this pattern, breathe deeper and with awareness. Breathe through your nose for 4 seconds and out through your nose for 8 seconds – try it now. If you get an audience to do this you can feel the calm descend on the room!

Drink water

Make sure you have got plenty of still water on the stage and maybe just at the side of the stage before you go on too. Go to the loo beforehand (sorry it's an honest book!) and drink a little water before you go on. As I said previously, mid-talk use the water as a way of pausing too, take a break, take a sip then carry on, it is good for you and thc audience won't mind.

Alcohol?

People often ask me about drinking alcohol before they speak. "Should I drink before I speak?" – should I have a little bit of 'Dutch courage' as they say? My answer is always a simple – no! Absolutely not, no talk has ever gone better because people have had alcohol beforehand. Trust me. I once coached someone who was doing a sensitive speech and I helped to write a talk for him, I coached him and talked him through it all. Then he had 3 or 4 pints before he stood up, threw his notes away and just made it up on the spot, ignoring the plan and telling the stories that we had agreed he shouldn't tell! Doh! He managed to offend and upset quite a lot of people that day, it was a car crash speech. So, no, never drink alcohol before speaking. Sure, have a glass afterwards, but never beforehand.

Be comfortable in your own shoes

Literally. Don't wear brand new clothes or shoes when speaking. You want to be comfortable in what you are wearing you don't want to feel like things don't fit properly, you don't want shoes that are going to make your feet hurt or clothes that just don't feel right. Be comfortable in what you wear, it is as important as looking smart.

Deal with any objections beforehand

Quite a bit of anxiety comes from thinking about the possible objections to our content and the difficult questions that people might ask. It is perfectly natural for us to think about the possible fall-out from a challenge that we may bring, it is part of being a speaker. If we bring change, ask for change or upset unhelpful patterns that an audience has, even in a business pitch, we are challenging the norms that exist and bringing solutions to our clients' problems. From time to time I do 'train the trainer' sessions, helping the in-house trainers in a company or organisation to sharpen up their delivery skills. These are, if I'm honest, often one of the most challenging sessions that I do, as often there are 12 people in the room who communicate for a living being told how to communicate. Tricky! One of the main things that

I have learned to do is to pre-empt their questions and objections on paper and deal with them before I begin my delivery. It is a great habit to get into. Once you know the objections, challenges and sticking points and have an answer or referral for them, it helps you to relax more, increases your knowledge and lets you deal with things as they arise. You may not be able to answer every question or objection but you'll be better equipped than most and your anxiety will be reduced.

The 'who will be in the room' panic!

The imposter syndrome is very real. People in leadership roles often secretly wonder how they got to where they are and hope that no-one will find out that they aren't perfect, that they sometimes get angry/shout at the kids/kick the dog and stay in their pyjamas at the weekend until midday watching box sets on TV. One of the reasons that presentations are so scary for some people is that it kicks into this insecurity which is ramped up when they think about being 'on display' on stage, especially with people in the room that they feel are cleverer or more experienced than they are. There are very helpful books and blogs on this subject and chatting it through with someone may help too. As a presentation coach, the best advice I can give you is to own your talk. No-one has your personality, and your stories, therefore no-one can do the talk that you do. Own it, it is yours. The other way to reduce your stress on this matter is never to pretend that you know everything and have all the answers. I have seen people do this, especially the hard sell speakers[13]. Have the attitude of 'I'm telling my story and my take on this', instead of 'I have

13. You know, the ones who promise to make you a millionaire in 90 days without any evidence of it or anyone on stage who has actually become a millionaire because of their help!. There is a clue there somewhere!

all the answers and I know more than anyone else'. If you can't answer a question just admit it and maybe even refer a tough question to the other experts in the room. That may sound counter-intuitive but it can really work and shows that you're open to refer and learn too. Be confident in yourself and your story and you'll be ok. I have been in intense situations where 10 professional speakers are speaking for 10 minutes each to get new clients. Was it a competition? In some ways yes, but I treated it like any other talk and just presented my talk with my style and my story. That reduces anxiety significantly.

Practise in a good way

Remember when you practice and prepare make sure it's in a way that is good for you, make sure that it helps you to reduce your anxiety, not make it worse. Be kind to yourself.

Post talk help

When you are off-stage and finished, remember a few things to help you next time. There is no such thing as failure, there is only feedback. Failure is not a person it's just an event. Even if you just gave the worst talk in the world (which I'm sure isn't possible by the way!) you can say "Ok I have got some feedback from that, I know what went wrong, and I will do it better next time!" Just because someone gives you feedback, it might not be true, but even if it is, it can help you get better. It doesn't mean that you have failed or are a failure. Be good to yourself. The question that I have learned to ask myself after a talk is "Did I try my best?" not "Was I perfect?". "Did I do my best?". "Did I give it my best shot?" If the answer is yes then that's the best thing you can say to yourself, that is fantastic, that is much more positive and helpful than "was I perfect?" because the answer to that question is always no, I wasn't. I have never done a perfect talk in my life and neither will you. So ask yourself "Did I try my best?" you'll learn from it and do it even better next time.

You can reduce your anxiety by simply asking yourself the right questions.

Space for your notes

The S word!

As we near the end of my book we need to talk slides!

Note: When I talk about Slides or PowerPoint I mean any slide software. I use Apple Keynote mainly, you might use PowerPoint, Prezi, Haiku Deck, Sway, or the many different options out there. No matter what software you use, the same principles apply.

The power of bad slides is strangely addictive

The problem is that people can read a book like this, or come to a day-long presentation course and say (or secretly think) "I'll just use my old slides again" completely ignoring what they've been taught and experienced.

People get drawn back to their old, often Death-by-PowerPoint[14], slides like an gambler gets drawn back into the betting shop.

It sounds over-dramatic but it is true, I've seen it.

Great slides in a nutshell:

To get great slides you have to first of all **STOP** and ask the question, who are slides for?

Once you have answered that question it changes everything.

Slides are for your *audience*, they are not for you as a speaker, they are not a script or a crutch, they are for the *audience* and therefore you should design them with the *audience* in mind.

What would you like to see on slides as an audience member? I guarantee that it won't be loads of bullet points.

Bullets kill people and presentations

No one has ever laid on their death bed and said "you know, I wish I had seen more bullet points".

Bullet points are there because people have taken a PDF sales brochure and made it into slides and that's how they do their talks, they read out of their brochure, because that's what bad slides are.

Nobody likes them, the only bullet point I ever use is in a quiz I do during a long workshop situation. I don't ever use them for anything else – there are always alternatives to bullet points.

Use more images and less text

Don't just think about cutting and pasting, don't think about writing endless text.

14. 'Death-by-Powerpoint' = boring slides and endless bullets points that add nothing to the talk and act as a written script to the speaker. I'm sure you've seen it in action!

Use images. If you are in a business, use images of your customers who are happy with your product. If you work for a charity, show your charity in action, show what you do (you can always blur out faces and show people without showing their faces, there are a lot of creative ways of making things anonymous) but ultimately get more full screen images on your slides, that is what people want – less text more quality images.

Ask

Once you have learned to prepare and deliver presentations in a different way, before each one always stop to ask the question "Do I need slides?"

Most people never ask that question.

Most talks can benefit from **good** slides but some talks just don't need slides at all.

When I have spoken at events or where it wasn't possible to have slides, it wasn't the end of the world. Even though I like good slides, I still delivered well.

Restraint is required

Don't do the default.

Don't just do what you have always done. If you have always used slides, you have to stop and challenge yourself, "even though this is what I have always done – I am not going to do it that way anymore" – walk away.

That's what this book is for, to get you away from your default bad habits and into something new and creative to help you to engage an audience. So, don't just do the default, don't open PowerPoint then click 'new document' and start doing title and bullet points, title and bullet points. You can change your default action, read the preparation section and go analogue first.

You are a designer

Everything you put on a slide is a design choice, the font, the size of the font whether it's bold, italic or regular. The background too. Whether you put a photograph on there or not. These are all design choices so take responsibility, whether you like it or not you are a designer, so learn some basic design rules.

The easiest rule to learn is to **'think billboard not document'**, so design slides as if they were billboards not an A4 Word document like most people do. You design the slides for the person on the back row, can they see your slides? If they can your design will be simpler and clearer.

The big problem

The issue isn't that slides have become harder to make, it is the opposite, they have become easier to make and that's our fundamental problem. In the 70's and 80's to have a transparency/slide done you would have to design it, have it sent away and then developed. Or you'd have had to have an acetate/overhead projector slide, tape a frame around it, write on it and do some coloured hand drawing on it! Now it's so easy we just open up PowerPoint and just start putting text on it instantly.

Just because it's easy it doesn't mean that we should do it.

The big challenge

If you are a slide addict then I challenge you, take a risk.

I dare you to speak without slides next time. If you have never 'presented naked' in your life then I dare you to do it, speak without slides, but keep your clothes on! Every now and again I go 'sans slides' myself to keep fresh and to help me understand that it is about me engaging with an audience, it is about connection, it is not about my fancy fonts and the nice photograph I have just found.

If you want to see a more in-depth and full colour way to make your slides better, bigger and bolder, feel free to look at my book 'PowerPoint Surgery'. I also have an online course with 4+ hours of teaching from myself, including exercises and lots of extras, that's available now from PowerPointSurgery.com – more information about my books are at the end of this book.

Space for your notes

Frequently asked questions

These FAQ's are taken from real sessions that I have delivered, there are many more that I get asked but most have been covered earlier in this book. If you have one I haven't answered please do get in touch via twitter it is @leejackson

People often ask me:

How do I deliver dull content?

Dull content is made better in three ways. Firstly thin down your content into the key things the audience really needs. Secondly tell stories about the content and how it relates to the real world using other techniques to be more interesting, i.e. moving around the stage, asking questions and using your voice well. And thirdly give them a more comprehensive PDF or handout at the end for the finer details. Our job as a speaker is to be the filter, we have to filter our content and only deliver what the audience needs.

How do I engage reluctant audience members/ delegates?

There are many ways to do this but I would say that brief eye contact with everyone in the room works wonders and in the preparation stage always think that you need to change focus every 3-5 minutes. Remember your talk is not a whole entity, it is little chunks of content strung together, so make those chunks varied and different to increase engagement of everyone.

When I am in a workshop situation, how do I get shy people to speak up in the group?

I always watch a group closely at the beginning of a session and notice who is chatty and who stays quieter. Then a great technique is to get them to talk to each other first and then feedback to the group – this breaks the silence and encourages people to speak up. Also, if working in a small group I try to learn everyone's name and deliberately ask people by name to answer questions or give feedback. I try to foster a "we are all in this together" and "we will all engage and interact" attitude for my workshops, that breaks down a lot of barriers.

Should I use notes? Shouldn't I use notes?

There is nothing wrong with using notes while speaking. BUT, if the notes become a crutch for you or a distraction to the audience as they flap around you need to go to another strategy. In smaller rooms notes can be placed on a desk. I sometimes use blank note cards (but not with a piece of string or old school 'treasury tag' holding them together!) To be honest most people know their talk and they just worry so use notes. A friend of mine used to use copious amount of notes then on stage one day he dropped them all and he just carried on. He never used them again after that because he realised he didn't need them.

How do I keep to time when I am speaking upfront?

If you know that you have 30 minutes then plan and practise to fill that time but allow flexibility as sometimes you have to shorten your talk, I have to often. I also use a presentation timer app on my iPhone or iPad and set it to countdown to the allotted finish time, then no matter what time I start I still know my end time. As I've said, no one likes you to over-run unless in exceptional circumstance like a fire alarm interruption (yup, that has happened to me too!).

What's the difference between speaking, training and facilitation?

This is a tricky one and could get me into trouble. I think a couple of differences are clear. Training is usually much longer than speaking and with fewer people. Also often trainers use other people's material i.e. they teach leadership using the work of leading experts and authors, whereas a speaker on the whole uses (or should use) their own stories and material and only refers to others in passing. Facilitation is more like directing traffic, you are there to steer and guide other people's work, input and comments, you are supposed to be almost invisible. Speaking is, on the whole, for a shorter time, and more cut-to-the-chase. A keynote speech should have lots engagement but often very little interaction from the audience.

Do you have any advice to help me do a good 'elevator pitch' / short 30 second talk to do while introducing myself at a business networking event?

Be different, everyone else will say "Hi I'm…And I work for…And we do…". Make people smile, maybe tell them something they don't know about you and tell them how you can help them and not just what you do. I once heard a solicitor say this "Hi I'm…I work for… And we just do everything that every other solicitor does". I nearly fell off my chair! Getting them to remember you is key. I have used many lines over the years depending what I'm there for, including my gag about that famous TV presenter from the 80's e.g. "Hi I'm Lee and I know I look a bit like Keith Chegwin, I help people to be more authentic and less nervous when they have to present." That little gag about Keith Chegwin is enough to break the pattern of the boring ones they've just heard. They smile, they remember me and I have more conversations. Try a few out and see what gets results and matches your personality.

How do I develop new content on my chosen subject?

The best way to develop content is to find the way your brain works best (see the preparation section) and use the particular techniques that work well to develop your material. Use your expertise to write down your knowledge, as well as to collect your own stories and anecdotes. Then be very harsh with it and filter it well. Comedians often use a ranting technique. They get up and just rant away, recording what they say and then picking it apart afterwards. That might work quite well for you too, start talking about your subject while standing up (for more energy) with your phone on record and just go for it and you can then pick apart what you've said and may well uncover a gem or two of content to use. Give it a go.

What happens if you lose your place in your talk? How do you get back to where you want to be?

Remember that the audience doesn't know what you don't tell them, so if you lose your place just try and carry on and move on to the next chunk of content. Let your brain do what is does well – connect the dots. Eventually you will know what you missed out and may choose to drop it in later or just keep going. Having some brief notes or cards nearby may help you to find your place again too. I often have notes nearby but rarely use them unless I just want to be steered back in the right direction. They are more like road signs to me than notes to read out. Often people lose their place because they are trying to learn the whole speech as a script, I advise against that as it is very hard to make that sound relaxed and authentic. If you don't try to learn it you won't lose your place as much, you just might hit the odd speed bump and have to make little adjustments along the way, not completely stop, crash and burn.

How do I amend my style for different types of audiences? In other words, how do I do the same talk to adults in business, teenagers in school, or even primary schools?

Research is key here, find out about your audience and make sure that your content hits their expectations. Often the same content can be delivered to different audiences but the key is to adjust the way you say stuff and its application. I have done a similar talk to business leaders as I have done in schools but the stories I choose are slightly different. The delivery style differs and the way I get the content to 'land' is different.

i.e. for a school I might talk about how their mindset matters to get them through their revision and exams, whereas in a business context I would talk about how it helps them to become more resilient in the workplace. Same content, different applications. Like anything else you have to try it out, see what works, ask for advice.

In a nutshell...

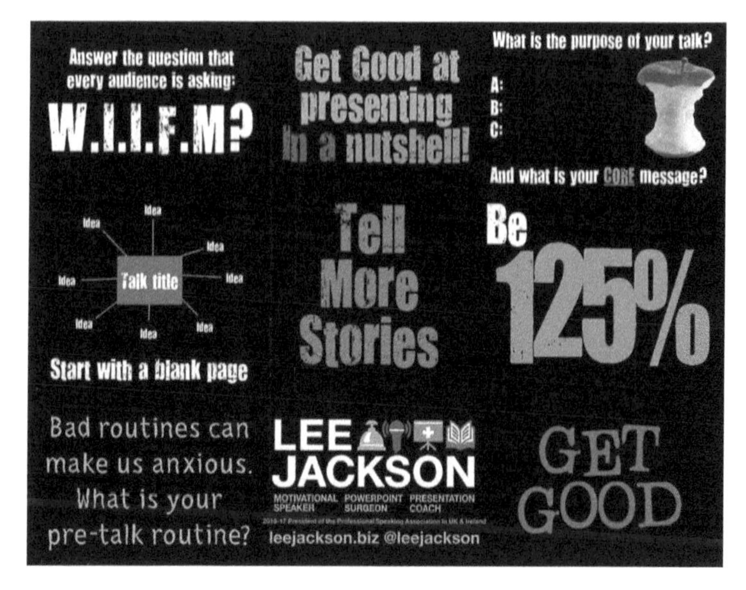

(Full colour printable version available free from: http://bit.ly/GetGoodPresExtras)

Space for your notes

Superman v Muhammad Ali

Muhammad Ali was probably the greatest sports star of all time and at the height of his career he was getting ready to fly to New York. Everyone on the aeroplane was excited, they were whispering "Muhammad Ali is on the aeroplane, Muhammad Ali is on the aeroplane". His entourage was there with him as he sat in first class as 'the champ', the greatest sports star, and possibly the greatest entertainer of all time. He was in his prime. The aeroplane was just about to take off and the cabin crew did that weird thing that they do, where they walk up and down the aisle and look at your crotch! They are checking that everyone had their seatbelt on and as she passed Muhammad Ali she noticed he didn't have his seatbelt on.

So she whispered in his ear "Ahem. Excuse me Mr. Ali can you put your seatbelt on please?" Muhammad Ali said "Superman doesn't need a seatbelt!".

Everyone was impressed and started writing down the quote to use later. Then stewardess very calmly and politely leaned over and whispered into his ear "Yes Mr. Ali, but Superman does not require an aeroplane".

Speaking can be a solo and lonely pursuit, but it doesn't have to be, you can be part of a team too. We don't have to be the person who is on their own the whole time 'saving the world' with their talks then driving four hours home alone every night. Learn in front of others, perform your talks to others to get feedback and to sharpen yourself up.

Try the PSA (thepsa.co.uk/join), or other speaking associations or groups.

Don't aim to be Superman or Superwoman – we are not all-powerful aliens from another planet landing on earth to deliver talks to an unsuspecting audience. Be a people person, own your stories, connect to the audience, use the good feedback and get better every time.

Enjoy the journey of speaking, enjoy your work, enjoy making a difference.

Thank you for engaging.

Appendix

Some helpful and fun extras,

Don't forget the resource page too – http://bit.ly/GetGoodPresExtras

Busting the Mehrabian (or 7%) Myth

Often quoted in talks, text books and, sadly, many presentation skills books is the study from 1967 by Dr. Albert Mehrabian.

The study gave the now famous figures that:

7% of our communication is conveyed by words,

38% by our tone of voice

and

55% by our body language.

This study is so often repeated, so badly used out of context and misquoted that Dr. Mehrabian himself has asked people to stop using it incorrectly!

He says himself on his website (http://www.kaaj.com/psych/smorder.html)

"Please note that this and other equations regarding relative importance of verbal and nonverbal messages were derived from experiments dealing with communications of feelings and attitudes (i.e. like-dislike). Unless a communicator is talking about their feelings or attitudes, these equations are not applicable"

In other words – this often quoted study has nothing at all to do with public speaking, it is about personal likability in conversations about feelings and attitudes.

Of course, in speaking, body language is important and yes, tone of voice is key. We have discussed these in this book **but** words are very important indeed.

If only 7% of communication was about the words we speak then we would hardly ever have to learn a foreign language.

There is a great little video on this subject on Youtube, the link is on the resources page mentioned on the previous page.

Here is the pre-talk techie info I send to my clients, it really helps the event organisers, why not make your own?

Equipment and Technical Requirements for Speaker Lee Jackson

The following information is learned from experience and helps to make my presentations / workshops run smoothly and prevent those 'last minute panics'.

In terms of I.T. related equipment for the presentation, I deliver a full multi-media presentation from my own Apple Mac laptop (I have the video adapter from my mac to a VGA/HDMI).

I will need the following equipment to be provided, in order for me present at my best:

I often use my own laptop for slides, so it needs it to be positioned on the stage/front of hall near to where I will be presenting (on a table please, not a music stand – don't ask!).

A bright, good quality data projector to connect to my laptop (I can supply my own if needed), projected onto a large enough screen that everyone has full view of it.

Sound from my laptop is needed too, so the stereo 'headphone out' from my laptop needs to connect to a full sound system (or good quality amp for smaller venues, I can supply my own if needed).

If the size of the venue and number of participants requires it (i.e over 30 people) a good quality wireless lapel microphone is required to amplify my voice, again, I can supply my own if needed.

Other (non – I.T.) stuff:

Plenty of pens for delegates and a Flipchart (if delivering a workshop/ cafe style session).

A power extension lead.

Two small bottles of still water.

For my education clients – a few treats / rewards to give away appropriate to your event.

A small / medium size table to put some props / laptop on.

If you are unable to provide the above set-up, please confirm this with me or my agent as soon as possible, so arrangements can be made. Thank you.

Funnies

Many years ago for another project on speaking in a school context I started collecting stories of talks that had gone wrong, here are a few for your enjoyment!

I'm sure you may have heard a few too, feel free to send them on.

Flowers

"I heard the story of a youth worker who was taking a school assembly along the lines of 'seeing is believing'. Being determined to outdo other youth workers using the same old illustrations, he went for it! He laced a bunch of 'edible' daffodils heavily with tomato ketchup and proceeded to devour the whole daffodil in front of the group. Unfortunately what he didn't realise was that only the coloured petals are vaguely 'edible' (do not try this!) and he must not eat the greenery on the flower, which is often poisonous. So with the greenery, petals and the tomato ketchup combined he promptly threw up all over the floor, at which point in the nervous spasm he also knocked over the tomato ketchup bottle which smashed splattering tomato ketchup and vomit up the walls and the students!"

Always check the health and safety of your props!

Cupboard love

"At a youth talk we showed part of a sex education video. To add to the atmosphere we turned the lights out. During the night a parent walked in, saw we were watching a sex ed video and promptly walked out again. No one could concentrate for the rest of the session because, instead of going out of the door, the parent had walked into a cupboard! Obviously too embarrassed to come out again, they had spent the next 20 minutes standing in the broom cupboard with the light off. We had to send everyone out of the room before the said parent could be coaxed out again!"

Always check your exits!

Tied up!

"I once did an talk in front of a whole school where I'd cut a teacher's tie off with a pair of scissors just below the knot in the middle of the talk. Naturally the teacher had been carefully prepared in advance and provided with an old tie from a charity shop, but unfortunately my colleague had passed the tie to the wrong teacher and I cut his 'real' tie off in front of everyone!"

Always choose the right volunteers!

I bumped into the head teacher

"After delivering a talk in a school I got into my VW van in the car park and started to drive slowly away. The head teacher was walking to her car too when a pupil ran around the corner and bumped into her, knocking her glasses off her face and onto the tarmac. She knelt down to pick up her glasses without realising they had fallen into the path of my moving van. Just after I saw her lunge in front of my van I heard a bump! I had knocked over the head teacher who had booked me to speak on my way out of her school! Fortunately, she brushed herself off and went on her way, glad that her glasses were not broken! I was just relieved that I hadn't killed anyone!"

Always drive slowly and carefully when approaching or leaving the venue!

Some example written intros from Pro Speakers

Use these as a way of seeing how to be introduced by the MC.

Find the right fit for you and use the technique shown earlier in this book.

Intros used here with the very kind permission of the owners.

"He's a qualified butcher, baker and most recently a Candlestick Maker, a former professional lookalike, I have no idea what he's going to talk about, let's hope that he does…please welcome Adam Harris"

"Our next speaker started his first business aged just 12 years old. Standing here today at 27, he has more business experience than most people twice his age. He's worked with hundreds of businesses in the UK and across the world, helping them to get better results from their marketing. Please welcome Nathan Littleton"

"Rohit Talwar is a global futurist who has worked with leaders in over 70 countries on 6 continents helping them to anticipate and create the future. He was profiled by the UK's Independent as one of the top ten global future thinkers and has received a 'stickiest guru' award. Rohit has been a stand-in for Arnold Schwarzenegger (not a body double) and was recently on Interpol's most wanted list. Please welcome Rohit Talwar"

"Please welcome your short, yet funny MC Emma Stroud."

"Our next speaker has been working under cover. In the last 12 months she has attended four speaker conventions on four continents; she's witnessed countless keynote performances and breakout sessions secretly observing and analysing the speakers. And of all those speakers, there were just four who really stood out. Today for the very first time she will reveal to you who they are, what they did and what you can learn from them to help you speak stronger. Please welcome Mel Sherwood."

"The next speaker went to Oxford because he wanted to join the Footlights Revue, the legendary comedy club that's produced British comedy heroes from Monty Python and The Goodies to Mel & Sue. Then when he got there he discovered that the Footlights is at Cambridge. Ever since then he's been walking through the wrong door and saying sorry. He was once in a comedy group with Steve Coogan, and now he helps executives to be more interesting. Please welcome, Tony Coll."

How to deliver an Assembly in Schools

Over the years many people have asked me for my advice on doing an 'assembly' or short talk in their local school. Many people have to do them and they can seem pretty scary. Here is a tried and tested formula and some general advice about this very specific speaking niche as a visitor in schools.

Before I was a 'professional keynote' speaker, most of the short assemblies I have done in schools have included some sort of game or short activity which will require volunteers. The reason I do that is not because the game is significant, although often the games are related to the subject, however loosely. But if you get young people or their friends helping out with a game, they get a little bit of stardom that will hold their attention for the few minutes afterwards when you deliver a short talk.

I reckon you have to earn your right to speak with young people, no matter who you are.

I believe most schools talks should be based around prizes! It is a great incentive. So if you get volunteers in assembly make sure they have a prize. Even if it is a competition and somebody wins, make sure that all of the volunteers get a prize as well. It is important to value them not as winners and losers but as people. How you treat volunteers and people in schools is just as important as the things that you say.

I was taking an assembly in front of 600 pupils once, the whole of key stage 3 was there (11-14 year olds), and I asked for two volunteers for a quiz. All the hands shot up as usual from the younger pupils and I chose a girl and a boy. Because they were a fairly new year group I didn't know them very well, and as I chose the boy and he stood up I suddenly noticed that all the teachers started talking to each other and there was a lot of mumbling. As he got to the front it was apparent the lad I had chosen had special needs. All the teachers and pupils were watching me very carefully to see how I dealt with him. Because it was a quiz I did go through it with him very carefully, but he wasn't able to answer any questions and the girl won easily. It was so important that I honoured this lad, who had had the guts to put his hand up and come out in front of all the people in his year, so I made sure he got a prize and a big round of applause afterwards.

Choose volunteers carefully. If you get no hands going up then ask one of the teachers to choose for you, and that will remove any embarrassment and any of the concerns you may have over the volunteers. I must admit though I tend to live a little bit more by the seat of my pants and like to see what will happen. Get people to give a round of applause as the volunteers come out to the front and make sure they get a round of applause at the end, so they go out feeling really good about themselves.

Be aware that if you do decide to do a game in assembly, not all games that people do in youth groups are appropriate for schools! Large banana splits, egg-related games and other mad things are not appropriate for school mainly because of the mess and the nightmare you have afterwards cleaning it up.

If I have got a lot of equipment to set up I often ask the students to help me. They usually like to be involved. The time before and after assemblies is just as important as the assemblies themselves, so be aware of the way you treat people as you set up and pack things away.

Instead of talking about a random concept, it is much better to make it personal and talk about your life, your job, your dog, the sports that you play, TV that you watch, and the things that happen in your family life. I was doing an assembly once and decided to add an illustration I hadn't planned on. I started talking about me dating Clare before we were married. I looked across the assembly hall and realised all eyes were transfixed on me! I discovered the power of personal story that day. There is a danger, of course, that you could share too much, so be careful, but it is much more interesting to young people than 'this book says this…'.

Everyone has their own style, but the following is a general pattern that I used to work to when doing short school assemblies. (Remember in secondary schools you usually get 5 to 10 minutes and 10 to 25 minutes in primary school – but do check!)

1. Intro yourself (and team if needed)

2. A game, demo, prop illustration or video clip

3. A short talk – keeping it to one main point

4. A one-line conclusion / challenge (ideal for if the bell rings!)

Expect the unexpected as a school visitor and be flexible. I make sure I plan a ten-minute assembly for a secondary school, but I have sometimes been given just two or three minutes, so something has to go! Be yourself, be respectful to all, finish on time for the bell and enjoy the opportunity.

Emergency Talk Panic Station!

"But what do I do if I haven't got much time to plan a talk Lee?!"

An easy way to plan a talk when time is tight.

Think 3x3.

What are your 3 main points?

Then say 2 things about your 3 main points, in the rows.

Then add an intro and an outro, and you're sorted.

So, say if you are planning for a 1 hour talk you might have 15 things that you have planned but you could get that down to 3 main points.

It's a nice technique to use, make 3 main points then 2 further points on the 3 points. So, 9 points overall, one could be a video, one a story etc.

This simple structure often helps to focus when we have limited time to prepare.

See next page…

Simple Presentation Planning Sheet.

Don't plan a talk on your computer, close it down, take some time out and work through this sheet first. It'll be worth it.

What is the purpose of your talk?

What do you want them to walk away with?

What is in it for them?

What are your 3 main points?

Main point	Supporting content i.e. stories, case studies, video, data etc.	Supporting content i.e. stories, case studies, video, data etc.
1		
2		
3		

copyright @leejackson

Presentation Skills…	Jargon	Acronyms without explanation	Too much content	Talking too fast
Presentation Skills…	Random story	Projector shining on presenter	Boring intro	Over running the allotted time
Blank row to add your own…		**Bad Talk Bingo!**		
Slides…	Times New Roman font!	Comic Sans font!!	Low resolution photograph	More than 3 bullet points
Slides…	Reading from the slides	"These aren't my slides"	"you can't see this so I'll read it"	Dull corporate template

Take this to your next conference. If you get a full house tweet it to @leejackson #badtalkbingo #getgood :)

Bad Talk Bingo!

(A PDF of this and the planning sheet is available from the resource page, visit: http://bit.ly/GetGoodPresExtras)

Also by Lee Jackson...

'Powerpoint Surgery' The book

'Powerpoint Surgery' Online Masterclass – http://bit.ly/PowerpointSurgeryMasterclass

'Getting Your Teenagers Through Their Exams'

'How To Enjoy And Succeed At School And College'

Also Lee is a contributor to many other books including:

'The Business Of Professional Speaking' (Panoma Press)

GCSE Revision Study Skills (Collins)

N5 & Higher Study Skills (Collins)

You can find more info and buy them now directly from:

Lee's Amazon.co.uk authors page – http://bit.ly/LeeJacksonAuthorsPage

Lee's Web-Shop – http://bit.ly/LeeJacksonWebShop

Space for your notes

Lightning Source UK Ltd.
Milton Keynes UK
UKHW021820060619
343997UK00021B/399/P

9 780956 754288